HEGEL AND THE PRIMACY OF POLITICS.
TAMING THE WILD BEAST OF THE MARKET

DIEGO FUSARO (Turin, Italy, 1983) teaches History of Philosophy at the Institute for Higher Strategic and Political Studies, Milan, Italy. He studies the philosophy of history and the structures of historical temporality, particularly focusing on Fichte, Hegel, Marx and the German 'history of concepts'. He is the director of the *I Cento Talleri* series on philosophy published by Il Prato and is the editor of the online project *La filosofia e i suoi eroi* (Philosophy and its heroes - www.filosofico.net). He founded the association and review *Interesse Nazionale* (National Interest - www.interessenazionale.net). Among his most recent books are *Bentornato Marx!* (2009), *Essere senza tempo. Accelerazione della storia e della vita* (2010), *Coraggio* (2012), *Minima mercatalia. Filosofia e capitalismo* (2012), *Idealismo e prassi. Fichte, Marx e Gentile* (2013), *Il futuro è nostro* (2014), *Fichte e l'anarchia del commercio* (2014), *Antonio Gramsci* (2015), *Pensare altrimenti* (2016), *Marx, again!* (The Pertinent Press, 2017), *The Place of Possibility* (The Pertinent Press, 2017) and *Marx, Epicurus and the Origins of Historical Materialism* (The Pertinent Press, 2018). He writes for the Italian newspapers *La Stampa* and *Il Fatto Quotidiano* and makes frequent appearances on Italian TV, sharing his political analyses with the general public. Whereas Enrico Galavotti, in his *Esegeti di Marx* (2015), describes Diego Fusaro as 'the rising star of contemporary Italian Marxist philosophy', Fusaro defines himself as an 'independent disciple of Hegel and Marx'.

HEGEL AND THE PRIMACY OF POLITICS
Taming the Wild Beast of the Market

Published by
P3rtınənt Press
an imprint of
Oxford Legal Publishing Limited
www.thepertinentpress.co.uk
OXFORD

P3RTINƏNT PRESS
focuses on and aims to further study and knowledge in
philosophy, history, cultural studies, and theology.

P3rtınənt Press®
is a registered trademark

Published in the United Kingdom by Oxford Legal Publishing Limited

Translated by Steven Cenci.
Picture on the cover (depicting Hegel) by Davide Deidda.

First published 2018 by Oxford Legal Publishing Limited

British Library Cataloguing in Publication Data
Data Available

Oxford Legal Publishing Limited
is registered in England as No. 10898419
at the following address:
52 Cornmarket Street
Oxford OX1 3HJ

Printed in the United Kingdom

ISBN: 978-1-912142-21-7

Diego Fusaro

HEGEL AND THE PRIMACY OF POLITICS

Taming the Wild Beast of the Market

Translated by
Steven Cenci

P3rtınənt Press
OXFORD

CONTENTS

HEGEL AND THE PRIMACY OF POLITICS

Taming the Wild Beast of the Market

'I am delighted to learn from various sources that your efforts for a successful formation of young men are bearing the best of fruits. It is admittedly necessary in this extravagant age for there to be a centre that may irradiate a doctrine capable of favouring a life theoretically and practically. It is true that empty heads will not be prevented from indulging in vague ideas and sonorous verbiage. But good heads suffer from it as well, since in recognising false methods in which they have been ensnared since youth they withdraw back in themselves, become abstruse, or dogmatic'.

(Goethe, letter to Hegel, 7 October 1820)

1

WELCOME BACK HEGEL! THE DIALECTICAL RELATION BETWEEN ONTOLOGY AND TEMPORALITY

'The series of configurations that consciousness goes through along its journey is, in reality, the detailed history of the cultural development of consciousness in its elevation to Science'.

(Georg W. F. Hegel, *Phenomenology of Spirit*)

'Interpreting Hegel means taking a stand on all the philosophical, political, and religious problems of our century'.

(Maurice Merleau-Ponty, *Sense and Non-Sense*)

Of all the philosophers of the Western tradition, Hegel seems to be the most dissonant with respect to our time: even more so than Marx, who, as the subject of a ceaseless exorcism that obsessively declares him dead in the hope of killing him off for good,[1] may still be *presentable* before the new world order, at the condition that, however – as Slavoj Žižek reminds us – he is taken in *decaffeinated* form,[2] stripped of his anticapitalistic *pathos* and of his revolutionary-type of natural political expressivity, and presented instead as the innocuous theoretician of globalisation,[3] and as the secret thinker of the Liberals' eternal dream that is the extinction of the State.[4] On his part, Hegel does not seem to be compatible in any way with our *Zeitgeist*. However, it would be incorrect to interpret today's antipathy towards Hegel – ubiquitously present at every philosophical and political *latitude* – as a mere subjective opinion or as a simple philosophical choice among the many available on the market of *Weltanschauungen* (*world visions*).

Instead, it comprises a unitary *social fact* – as formulated by Émile Durkheim,[5] – which is representative of the *spirit*

1 Jacques Derrida, *Spectres of Marx* (New York: Routledge, 1994).

2 Slavoj Žižek, *First As Tragedy, then As Farce* (London: Verso, 2009); Žižek, *In Defense of Lost Causes* (London: Verso, 2008).

3 See, for example, the 'decaffeinated' image of Marx proposed by Jacques Attali, *Karl Marx, ou l'Esprit du Monde* (Paris: Fayard, 2005).

4 See Pierre Rosanvallon, *Le Capitalisme Utopique* (Paris: Seuil, 1979) and Bernard Chavance, *Marx et le Capitalisme. La Dialectique d'un Système* (Paris: Nathan, 1996).

5 Emile Durkheim, *The Rules of Sociological Method* (New York: Free Press, 1982).

of the time: such *social fact* takes quite heterogeneous forms, over a broad spectrum of positions ranging from irony *à la* Rorty,[6] typical of those who embrace philosophy as one literary genre amongst many, to the postmodernist trends that reduce philosophical dialogue to a civil but non-veritative conversation, and that therefore see Hegel as an *naturaliter* authoritarian thinker (if not directly as a totalitarian enemy of *open society*),[7] to the apt delegitimisation of the *thought of totality* in favour of the *thought of the difference à la* Deleuze,[8] and finally, to the hysteria of those who radicalise their antipathy with slogans such as *We spit on Hegel*.[9] Indeed, it might even be said that the constant factor of our time is, at the philosophical level, the abandonment of the Hegelian dialectic in all its aspects.[10]

A hypothesis may thus be advanced, of which the following text will comprise an attempt of demonstration: the *organised hatred* towards Hegel is the quintessential expression of today's absolute-totalitarian capitalism, which sees in the Stuttgart philosopher – and not without reason – a thinker who is completely incompatible with its own global structuring. Hegel's incompatibility

6 Richard Rorty, *Philosophy and the Mirror of Nature* (Princeton: Princeton University Press, 1979).

7 Karl R. Popper, *The Open Society and Its Enemies* (London: Routledge, 1945).

8 Giles Deleuze, *Rhizome* (Paris: Minuit, 1976).

9 Carla Lonzi, *Sputiamo su Hegel* (Rome: Editoriale Grafica, 1970).

10 Jérôme Lebre, *Hegel à l'Épreuve de la Philosophie Contemporaine: Deleuze, Lyotard, Derrida* (Paris: Ellipses, 2002).

with today's neoliberal order is especially evident from the threefold fact that he *a)* thematises the concept of progressive dialectical attainment of self-consciousness by humanity in its process of emancipation and of universalisation of freedom (*Phänomenologie des Geistes*),[11] *b)* develops a *philosophical science* of totality ontologically apprehended and axiologically evaluated (*Wissenschaft der Logik*), persistently refusing to reduce philosophy to *ancilla scientiae*, and *c)* resolutely rejects the view of the capitalistically structured world, which regards the *civil society* of the egoistic-economic multitude of de-historicised, de-socialised, and abstract atoms, incessantly in competition with each other, as the moral foundation of the world, and counterposing this with a human community centred on the *Sittlichkeit* (*Grundlinien der Philosophie des Rechts*).[12]

For these reasons, the present age cannot but exorcise Hegel's presence;[13] an exorcism behind which, after all,

11 Jean Hyppolite, *Genesis and Structure of Hegel's Phenomenology of Spirit* (Evanston: Northwestern University Press, 1947).

12 On Hegel's incompatibility with the capitalistic structure, see Costanzo Preve, *Storia della Dialettica* (Pistoia: Petite Plaisance, 2006); with regards to the *Grundlinien*, see Lucio Cortella, *L'Etica della Democrazia. Attualità della Filosofia del Diritto di Hegel* (Genova: Marietti, 2011).

13 Karl Löwith, *From Hegel to Nietzsche: The Revolution in 19th Century Thought* (New York: Constable & Co., 1965) and Löwith, *Max Weber and Karl Marx* (London: Routledge, 2002). Löwith interprets the post-Hegelian philosophy in its entirety, from 1830 onwards, as a great process of dissolution of the Hegelian system and, more specifically, he subtly interprets it as the end of a pernicious delusion, giving way to the Weberian disenchantment of those who have learned to 'bear with virility' (*männlich ertragen*), without hopes or delusions, their own historical world. In a letter

is concealed a more general departure from philosophy as knowledge of the totality and from its axiological evaluation, simply replaced by forms of thought that, despite their irreducible diversity, all share as their common trait the absence of dialectics; and that, consequently, all result, even beyond their intentions, being functional to the present world order, the latter being founded on the *commodity form* and retaining its supremacy by preventing the registering and naming of contradictions that could lead to the proposition of alternative foundations. According to a theme that traverses most contemporary philosophical positions and that finds its programmatic formulation in Habermas' 1985 text *Der philosophische Diskurs der Moderne*,[14] Hegel is the first philosopher to have clearly thought the problem of modernity as *Grundfrage* (*fundamental question*), and, at the same time, the first philosopher that must be surpassed so as to be *modern* (Habermas) or *postmodern* (Lyotard).

We must now insist on the *necessity to re-start from Hegel, from his holistic and veritative view*, which is indispensable both for effecting a phenomenological reconstruction of the spirit of capitalism, and for demystifying the contradictions that infest our time. As suggested by Merleau-Ponty, 'interpreting Hegel means taking a stand on all the philosophical, political,

of September 1933 addressed to Gadamer, Löwith affirms that his interest in Marx lies exclusively in the fact that he sees him as the 'exponent of the collapse of Hegelian philosophy, the last one that still believed in itself, in philosophy as a philosophy'.

14 Jürgen Habermas, *The Philosophical Discourse of Modernity* (Cambridge: MIT Press, 1987).

and religious problems of our century',[15] refusing – and here lies the secret of idealism – to accept the world as a factual datum, as a dead positivity independent of human subjectivity. We must, however, dwell more closely on an apparent contradiction: the *Hegelian connection between truth and history* or, from a different perspective, between *eternity and temporality*.[16]

The apparent contradiction is encapsulated within the two different and, at first glance, irreconcilable definitions that Hegel provides with regards to philosophy. On the one hand, according to what is outlined in the 1821 *Grundlinien der Philosophie des Rechts*, 'philosophy is its own time apprehended in thoughts' (*ihre Zeit in Gedanken erfaßt*):[17] taking flight only at dusk, philosophy 'manifests itself through time only after Reality has completed its formative process and made itself ready'.[18] Hence the impossibility, for the individual, to look beyond his own historical horizon (*hic Rhodus, hic saltus!*).[19] On the other hand, in agreement with the program

15 Maurice Merleau-Ponty, *Sense and Non-sense* (Evanston: Northwestern University Press, 1964).

16 Christophe Bouton, *Temps et Esprit dans la Philosophie de Hegel (de Francfort à Iéna)* (Paris: Vrin 2000); Preve, *Hegel Antiutilitarista* (Rome: Settimo Sigillo, 2007).

17 Georg Wilhelm Friedrich Hegel, *Elements of the Philosophy of Right*, trans. by H. B. Nisbet (Cambridge: Cambridge University Press, 1991) (henceforth abbreviated to *GPR*), p. 23.

18 Ibid.

19 Adriaan Paperzak, *Philosophy and Politics. A Commentary on the Preface to Hegel's Philosophy of Right* (Dordrecht: Springer, 1987).

outlined in the *Wissenschaft der Logik*, philosophy is called upon to occupy itself, in completely opposite way, with *what is eternal,* thus, with what is removed from becoming and from the passing of time:[20]

> The philosopher has nothing to do with prophetic activity. With history, we are more concerned with what has been and with what is, while in philosophy we deal not only with what has been or only with what will be, but with what is and is eternally, thus with reason, and this is enough already to deal with.[21]

It is Hegel himself to emphasise the apparent aporetic aspect of the relation between eternity and historicity (between *what is eternally* and a *particular historical time*), showing the incompatible character between the two dimensions from the perspective of that *contradictio in adiecto* that *history of philosophy* seems to be:

> What is true is contained only in thought, and it is true not only today or tomorrow, but beyond all time, and in as far as it is in time, it is true always

20 For a study on the 'apparently' aporetic relation between temporality and eternity see Gaetano Rametta, *Il Concetto del Tempo: Eternità e Darstellung Speculativa nel Pensiero di Hegel* (Milan: Angeli, 1989).

21 Hegel, *Die Vernunft in der Geschichte* (Leipzig: Meiner, 1917), p. 200. This is Hegel's vexed answer to the question 'is the United States to be understood as the country of the future?', put to him by a student during one of his courses on the philosophy of history.

> and for every time. This is in contradiction with the belief that thought has a history.[22]

The contradiction between these two different determinations – eternity and historicity, and therefore between the two different definitions proposed for philosophy – is, for Hegel, only apparent: indeed, philosophy deals with what is and is eternally, and thus configures itself as a dialectical logic that is not mere method but is ontology, that is, fulfilled theory of being and of its immanent dynamics; and, at the same time, what is and is eternally never presents itself in its hyperuranic immutability (God before the creation of the world, according to the evocative image of the *Wissenschaft der Logik*),[23] but always manifests itself as temporally mediated in a concrete history, in temporal configurations and in precise historical contexts, in real spatio-temporally determined *Gestaltungen*.[24] The eternal truth of the Idea indeed consists in the process of development through time, in which it leaves-itself to then

22 Hegel, 'Lectures on the History of Philosophy' in *Werke*, trans. by E. S. Haldane (London: Kegan Paul, Trench, Trübner & Co, 1892) (henceforth abbreviated to *VGP*), Vol. 1, p. 38.

23 'The exposition of God as he is in his eternal essence before the creation of nature and of a finite spirit' (*die Darstellung Gottes, wie er in seinem ewigen Wesen vor der Erschaffung der Natur und des endlichen Geistes ist*): Hegel, *The Science of Logic*, trans. by G. Di Giovanni, (Cambridge: Cambridge University Press, 2010), (henceforth abbreviated to *WL*), p. 29; Fulvio Papi, *Lezioni sulla 'Scienza della Logica' di Hegel* (Milano: Ghibli, 2000).

24 Grazia Tagliavia, *La storia come Fenomenologia dell'Assoluto in Hegel* (Palermo: L'Epos, 1995); Christoph Johannes Bauer, *Das Geheimnis aller Bewegung ist ihr Zweck. Geschichtsphilosophie bei Hegel und Droysen* (Hamburg: Felix Meiner Verlag, 2001); Joseph McCarney, *Hegel on History* (New York: Routledge, 2000).

return-to-itself enriched by the adventures in the negative, in the specific form of 'a *becoming-other* which must be redeemed' (*ein Anderswerden, das zurückgenommen werden muß*), and which, for this reason, 'is a mediation' (*ist eine Vermittlung*).[25] This *unity of the logical-ontological level* with the *historical-temporal level* finds its most striking formulation in the *Vorrede* to *Phänomenologie*,[26] which clearly explains how what is eternally true, fully becomes so in its historical development, as the result of mediation, as the outcome of an imminent processuality of the truth-becoming process of the logical-ontological principle:

> *The true is the whole* (*das Wahre ist das Ganze*). However, the whole is only the essence that is fulfilled *through* its own development (*durch seine Entwicklung*). Of the Absolute, indeed, must be said that it is essentially a result, that only in the end it is what it truthfully is.[27]

The truth of the process does not depend solely on its development nor can it be historicistically levelled on it, as it is located on a logical-ontological plane that pre-exists development ('God before the creation of the

25 Hegel, *The Phenomenology of Spirit*, trans. by A. V. Miller (Oxford: Oxford University Press, 1977) (henceforth abbreviated to *PG*), p. 20.

26 Roberto Racinaro and Vincenzo Vitiello, *Logica e Storia in Hegel* (Rome: Edizioni Scientifiche Italiane, 1985); Sergio Landucci, *Hegel: la Coscienza e la Storia. Approssimazione alla 'Fenomenologia dello Spirito'* (Florence: La Nuova Italia, 1976).

27 *PG*, p. 20.

world') and that, furthermore, is fully realised only within it. Truth implies a process of mediation which unfolds through time and which finds its landing stage in the final result, since 'only in the end it is what it truthfully is' (*es erst am Ende das ist, was es in Wahrheit ist*).[28] By varying Hegel's expression, the true is the whole, but in the form of a *has-become*, as a result and as a totality that has reached fulfilment and that has transitioned through the scissions of the *ungeheure Macht des Negativen* (*immense power of the negative*), after having left the original *in-itselfness* and having lost itself in alienation, without the easy shortcuts of who – like Schelling – arrives at the conclusion as a 'shot out of a pistol'.[29] It is the very fact that the Idea unfolds processually and has fully become itself only when the process has reached its completion, to imply that it is immersed in time and it has its own *history*: in this resides the Hegelian discovery of historicity as *Seinsgrund* (*foundation of being*).[30] In this perspective, the expression of the *Phänomenologie*, which could seem cryptic if read out of context, acquires a precise meaning: '[...] the true is its own becoming, the circle

28 Ibid.

29 'That rapturous enthusiasm which, like a shot from a pistol, begins immediately with absolute knowledge, and makes short work of diverging points of view by declaring that it takes no notice of them', Ibid, p. 27.

30 This point has been highlighted by Herbert Marcuse, *Hegel's Ontology and the Theory of Historicity*, trans. by S. Benhabib (Cambridge: MIT Press, 1987); Marcuse shows how the binomial of being and time, after Hegel, is reconfigured in the unprecedented form by which being is, by its very nature, temporality.

that presupposes its end as its aim, having its end also as its beginning; and only by being seen through to its end, is it actual'.[31]

If once, the religious concept of Absolute relating to the monotheistic divinity that perfectly pre-existed historical development, presented itself as originary and completely transcendental, the equivalent concepts of *Absolute* and *Geist* formulated by Hegel must be interpreted as the outcome of an entirely historical and *one-worldly* dialectic, which however is not resolved in the negation of the transcendental sphere.[32] Indeed, the outcome of such a dialectic may not be simply deduced from the empirical succession of historical facts, often accidental and in any case never deducible from a logic *a priori*: on the contrary, it must always be conceived also in logical-ontological terms, according to the teachings of the *Wissenschaft der Logik*. In agreement with the analysis of the Christian Trinity that Hegel undertakes in the *Vorlesungen* on the *philosophy of religion*,[33] a God before the creation of the world is not simply a God in an authentic sense, because He exists only in the dialectical development of the three figures of the Trinity. This means that, as God does not exist separately from the creation of the world, so too the

31 'Es ist das Werden seiner selbst, der Kreis, der sein Ende als seinen Zweck voraussetzt und zum Anfange hat, und nur durch Ausführung und sein Ende wirklich ist': *PG*, p. 18.

32 Marcello Monaldi, *Hegel e la Storia. Nuove Prospettive e Vecchie Questioni* (Naples: Guida, 2000), p. 51-60; and Preve, *Storia della Dialettica* (Pistoia: Petite Plaisance, 2006), p. 48.

33 Hegel, *Lectures on the Philosophy of Religion*, ed. by P. C. Hodgson (Berkeley: University of California Press, 1988) (henceforth abbreviated to *VPR*).

logical-ontological level of the Idea, which also retains its transcendental character irreducible to the historical dimension, does not exist without a necessary correlation with historicity, with the unfolding *sub species temporis*.[34]

Thus, in the Hegelian perspective – and here lies Hegel's *secret* – there is a productive balance between the *eternal element* (the universal validity of philosophy) and the *historical element* (the place of determination of philosophical truths, and therefore their particular genesis), in the context of a veritative conception of philosophy, in which *validity* (*Geltung*) is universal, and *genesis* (*Genesis*) is particular, and historically determined. In this way, at safe distance from the shallows of relativism, which dissolves historicistically the truth in the streams of becoming, and of the reduction of the veritative space of philosophy to mere ideology that reflects and sanctifies its own time, it is possible to *occupy oneself with the eternal by apprehending one's time in thoughts*, without there being contradiction between these two seemingly irreconcilable dimensions (eternity and temporality): the object of philosophical inquiry remains what it eternally is, but it finds its *determination* (*Bestimmung*) in a historically concrete society, and more precisely in the historical present in which the philosopher lives and acts. With perfect symmetrical coherence, as in the *Geschichte der Philosophie*, the most recent philosophy, thus the one that poses itself as the provisional landing stage for the unfolding process of the Idea, 'constitutes

34 Herbert Marcuse, *Reason and Revolution. Hegel and the Rise of Social Theory* (Oxford: Oxford University Press, 1941).

the result of all preceding philosophies' (*ist das Resultat aller vorhergehenden Philosophien*),[35] and is therefore 'the most developed, rich and concrete philosophy';[36] likewise, the most recent age, the historical present, becomes the privileged place for grasping the eternal in temporality, as 'the mirror of all history',[37] as the process in its entirety and in its actual dynamics.

This represents the highest point of establishing an ontology of the *social being*. Philosophy is called upon to operate in that specific and delicate dialectical relation that is established between the genesis of a philosophical constellation, which is always particular and historically determined, and its validity in terms of truth, which is instead always universal. In this way, there is no Descartes without the heterogeneous intersection of cultures typical of seventeenth century France, and there is no Socrates without that particular and unique historical set of conditions that saw the crisis of the Athenian democracy during and after the Peloponnesian war. Their particular philosophical elaborations, although historically determined in their genesis, show a universal validity, which transcends their historical time, even though they cannot exist without the latter. It is in this horizon of dynamic connection between truth and temporality, between universal validity and particular genesis, that the

35 Hegel, *Encyclopedia of the Philosophical Sciences*, trans. by A.V. Miller, (Oxford: Oxford University Press, 1990) (henceforth abbreviated to *EPW*).

36 Ibid.

37 *VGP*, Vol. 1, p. 41.

present work will focus on, in an attempt to demonstrate how philosophical systems and the categories of thought always present a historically determined genesis (in which the specific historical moment is reflected and, with it, the precise social context), without this, however, allowing them to be dismissed as *ideological*. On the contrary, they comprise as many moments of attainment of self-consciousness by humanity, which apprehends in thought its own time and, with it, the dynamics that Lukacs defined as 'the true self-realisation of man as a generic being'.[38]

38 György Lukács, *The Ontology of Social Being* (London: Merlin Press, 1980). The aporia from which we had started has therefore dissolved: in a perspective in which truth has the eternal as the father and temporality as the mother, the philosopher is called upon, for Hegel, to consider his own historical time and to grasp in it what is true and eternal within it, judging it in its entirety and according to criteria which cannot be deduced exclusively from the sphere of historicity; insofar as history is the unravelling of the Idea *sub specie temporis*, 'it is consistent with the concept of Spirit that *the development of history falls in time* (*fällt die Entwicklung der Geschichte in die Zeit*)', *VGP*; the 'history of the world' is the history of the temporal unfolding of the truth of the Idea, just as the 'history of philosophy' is the process of unravelling of the truth seized by the thoughts of the 'heroes' (*VGP*. p. 39) of thinking reason who constitute the 'holy chain' (*VGP*., p. 2) of the western canon. Hence the Hegelian thesis of the *coincidence of philosophy with its history*, a thesis centred on the belief that the succession of the philosophical systems that have come to develop coincides, albeit in an elastic way, with the succession of conceptual determinations of the Idea that unfolds over time, of the totality that articulates through a series of temporally configured degrees and moments. According to the Encyclopedia, *EPW*, § 13, 'in the philosophies that are manifest and that appear different, the history of philosophy shows, on the one hand, that it comprises *only a single philosophy in the different stages of its perfecting* (*nur eine Philosophie auf verschiedenen Ausbildungs-Stufen auf*), and, on the other, that the particular principles, each of which was the foundation of a philosophical system, are no other than the branches of one and only Whole' (*EPW*). Since 'history

The Hegelian perspective should be assimilated not only in virtue of its connection between the logical-ontological and the historical-temporal planes, but also of the one closely related to it, that between *philosophy and truth*. Against every type of Marxist (philosophy as an ideology), relativistic-nihilistic ('there are no facts, only interpretations') or scientistic (the reduction of truth to the operational field of science alone) reductionism, we must welcome Hegel's exhortation to retain an *autonomous space of philosophical knowledge* in connection with the plane of historicity. According to what is discussed in the sections dedicated to the *Doctrine of the Notion* in the *Wissenschaft der Logik*, philosophy must *apprehend truth in the dimension of historical temporality*, without however limiting itself to the mere factual narrative of events in their pure exterioriority as an accidental enumeration of opinions:

> If it is not the truth which is at issue but only history, as it is the case in pictorial and phenomenal thinking, *then we might as*

in general is therefore the development of Spirit in time, as nature is the development of the idea in *space*' (Hegel, *The Philosophy of History*, trans. by J. Sibree (New York: Dover Publications, 2004), p. 72), it follows that its historical present marks the 'highest' point of development of the process, the result of the millenary journey of the Idea and, consequently, it is necessary turning to in order to judge totality. Marx will reformulate this Hegelian principle by asserting that the most advanced society constitutes the truth of the preceding ones and must therefore constitute the starting point of their analysis, just as 'the anatomy of man provides a key to the anatomy of the ape': Karl Marx, *Grundrisse: Foundations of the Critique of Political Economy*, trans. by M. Nicolaus (London: Penguin Books, 1973).

> *well stay with the narration* (*so kann man allerdings bei der Erzählung stehenbleiben*) [...]. *But philosophy ought not to be a narrative of what happens, but a cognition of what is true in what happens, in order further to comprehend on the basis of this truth what in the narrative appears as a mere happening* (*aber die Philosophie soll keine Erzählung dessen sein, was geschieht, sondern eine Erkenntnis dessen, was wahr darin ist, und aus dem Wahren soll sie ferner das begreifen, was in der Erzählung als ein bloßes Geschehen erscheint*).[39]

In the Hegelian perspective, which is particularly timely if we consider the increasingly *absolutistic* claims of present scientism, philosophical truth is completely autonomous with respect to science. Unlike religion and art, which find a commonality with philosophy through the *object* (the truth of the whole, the Absolute), but differ in that they are separated from it by the *form of expression* (the weakened form of the religious *Vorstellung*,[40] and of the *sensory representation*,[41] operated by art are different and inferior to the power of the philosophical *Begriff*), science is constructed in a completely different way with respect to the *philosophische Wissenschaft*. It diverges from the latter not only by the expressive form, but also by the object, which in the case of science does not coincide with the

39 *WL*, p. 519.

40 *VPR*.

41 Hegel, *Aesthetics. Lectures on Fine Arts*, trans. by T. M. Knox (Oxford: Clarendon Press, 1975).

whole, but with the *empirical particular* isolated from the Whole and analysed by the abstract intellect. Indeed, they comprise spheres of knowledge with different and mutually irreducible fields, objects and forms of expression.

The arrogance of the present scientistic *theology* resides in the imposition of its own method and contents as the only *scientific* ones, and therefore as the only ones worthy of being pursued, reducing philosophical knowledge to mere abstract metaphysical *gossip* in a post-metaphysical world. In this way, knowledge stops at the conceptual figure of a *sense-certainty* (*sinnliche Gewissheit*),[42] haughtily masqueraded as the *non plus ultra* of knowledge. In Hegelian terms, philosophy – ἐπιστήμη τῆς ἀληθείας,[43] following Aristotle's definition – has as its own object the *truthful*, that is, the *concrete* totality grasped by *reason* through the *Begriff* and, consequently, it is *meta-physical* (μετὰ τὰ φυσικά), since the totality transcends the boundaries of mere empiricism. On its part, the object of science is what is *certain* with respect to the empirical plane, and therefore it is limited to portions of reality *abstracted* from the totality through the *abstrakter Verstand*. In agreement with Hegel's *Phänomenologie* and with Plato's *Republic* (according to which only 'he who views things in their totality is a dialectician'),[44] the *truthful* is only the whole, while the *part* can only be, each time, *certain*, *exact*, *wrong*, and so on. In Hegel's words, 'truth [...] can only deserve the

42 *PG*.

43 Aristotle, *Metaphysics* (Indianapolis: Hackett, 2016), 993b.

44 'Ὁ μὲν γὰρ συνοπτικὸς διαλεκτικός, ὁ δὲ μὴ οὔ', Plato, *Republic* (London: Penguin, 2012), 537c.

name if such truth has been engendered by philosophy',[45] with the consequence that 'without philosophy, other sciences – as much as they like to get along by ratiocination without it – are unable to keep alive, or to have any spiritual significance and truth in them'.[46]

Therefore, philosophical truth must not be understood as a *given* object to be gradually approached in the gnoseological space alone, uniting – according to the correspondence theory criticised by Heidegger,[47] – correspondence and coherence (from Aquinas' *adaequatio rei et intellectus*, to gnoseological realism, neo-Kantian first, positivist and Marxist later, to then give way to the present absolute primacy of empirical sciences). On the

45 *PG*, p. 67.

46 'To such questions as, When was Caesar born?, or How many feet were there in a stadium?, etc. a clear-cut answer ought to be given, just as it is definitely true that the square on the hypotenuse is equal to the sum of the squares on the other two sides of a right-angled triangle. But the nature of a so-called truth of that kind is different from the nature of philosophical truths', Ibid, p. 40.

47 Martin Heidegger, *Being and Time*, trans. by J. Stambaugh (Albany: State University of New York Press, 1996). According to Heidegger, modern metaphysical thought has produced the conception of a subject conceived no longer as a simple 'substratum' (*sub-jectum*), bearer of attributes and contingency, but as 'thinking I' (*ego cogitans*), pure, transcendental subject, a mere eye on the world, the foundation of truth as the place of its manifestation as an evident presence. The cognitive correlation between subject and object has thus given rise to a conception of *truth* as conformity or adaptation between language, thought and entity, *adaequatio rei et intellectus*. In opposition to this correspondence conception, Heidegger argues that being brings entities to light, it forms their background. In this sense, being is truth as ἀλήθεια, as movement of unveiling and of opening, such that truth is unveiled and by unveiling itself it opens in time.

contrary, philosophical truth implies a specific *relation of mediation between subject and object*, as pointed out by Fichte, Hegel and Marx himself.

More specifically, philosophical truth implies, on the one hand, that no object is given independently of the subject's consciousness and, on the other, that the subject formulates a global judgment on the whole, a judgment that is both cognitive and evaluative (in an inseparable unity of ontology and axiology). Even in this specific determination emerges the abyssal difference separating philosophy from science: this latter always implies knowledge of limited empirical portions of reality in the absence of a contextual moral evaluation, and this applies both to the *natural sciences* and to the *social sciences*, which are programmatically *value-free*, according to Max Weber's paradigm.

Against all appearances, the revival of Hegel's philosophy in the form of ontology of the social being constitutes the only possible starting point for a structural reaction to rampant absolute-totalitarian capitalism: not only because it allows to axiologically evaluate and to ontologically know the capitalistic totality, thus enabling a critical and anti-adaptive stance, but also because, from its original conception, philosophy has been animated by an uninterested contemplation that lies at a safe distance from the lust for utility and profit, instead identifying them as objects of critique, in this way revealing its affinity for the *act of giving*.[48] Philosophy is indeed connected with the

48 Jean-Luc Marion, *Being Given: Toward a Phenomenology of*

latter both in terms of gratuitousness (the much-deprecated *uselessness* of philosophy, or knowledge as an end-in-itself and freed from by the bond of *useful* servitude), and of the elements of surprise and wonder (in this respect, the θαυμάζειν, identified as the *engine* of philosophy already by both Plato and Aristotle,[49],[50] presents an extraordinary resemblance to the surprise that accompanies every act of giving). In virtue of its structure of *original givenness*, philosophical knowledge has been, ever since its Greek origins, a programmatic arrest of the *chrematistic* principle of the pursuit of profit and, at the same time, an iconoclastic act of reclaiming freedom through knowledge, regardless of the asymmetries of power and in defence of the community based on the just measure (from Diogenes' παρρησια to Spinoza's *libertas philosophandi*).[51]

Givenness (Stanford: Stanford University Press, 2002).

49 'This feeling of wonder shows that you are a philosopher, since wonder is the only beginning of philosophy': Plato, 'Thaetetus' in *The Dialogues of Plato* (New Haven: Yale University Press, 1984), 155d.

50 'It is through wonder that men now begin and originally began to philosophise': Aristotle, *Metaphysics*, 982b.

51 After all, the gratuitousness of the gift of the philosopher to the community is testified not only by the absence of a personal advantage that can be traced back to the laws of the *mos oeconomicus*, but also by the negative aspect of the frequent ingratitude with which the community repays him (the events surrounding Socrates, Bruno and Vanini are, in this respect, exemplary in their paradigmatic value). As a knowing that is an end in itself and, consequently, proudly 'useless' if we regard it as part of the instrumental and utilitarian aspect of the capitalistic cosmos, philosophy, since its inception, has broken the deadly chrematistic spell of the *do ut des* and operates what Husserl has defined as 'a sort of *epoché* of the practical life of interests'. Edmund Husserl, *Teleologie in der Philosophiegeschichte* (1936). One can then fully agree with Aristotle when he states that

Following these presuppositions, and by grafting Marx's thought onto Hegel's philosophical perspective, the theme of the present work is centred on the view of historicity as the place of humanity's *becoming-for-itself* and as the process of *man's becoming-man*,[52] that is, as the universal realisation of his ontological potentiality as ζῷον πολιτικὸν (sociable, political and communitarian animal) and as ζῷον λόγον ἔχον (animal endowed with reason, language and calculation of the just limit), according to an Aristotelian reorientation *lato sensu* of the two interconnected Marxian concepts of *Gemeinswesen* (*communitarian essence*), and *Gattungswesen* (*human essence*).[53,54] Even though it is an aspect often concealed by Marx himself and almost always removed by later Marxisms, Marxian thought is also established on a veritative foundation, outlined by Lukács and Preve:[55] the development of the essence of man, of his ontological structure as a sociable, communitarian, rational and structurally *multidimensional* animal (*das allseitig entwickelte Individuum*, according to *Das Kapital*),[56] corresponds to the general movement of history as a progressive approximation to the *conformity to mankind*

'although all other sciences are materially more necessary than this, none is superior'. Aristotle, *Metaphysics*, 983a.

52 Lukács, *The Ontology of Social Being*.

53 Karl Marx, 'On the Jewish Question' in *Early Writings* (New York: Penguin, 1992).

54 Preve, *Elogio del Comunitarismo* (Napoli: Controcorrente, 2006).

55 Ibid.

56 Marx, *Capital. A Critique of Political Economy*, trans. by B. Fowkes (London: Penguin Classics, 1990) (henceforth abbreviated to *DK*).

after the transition through the negative of capitalism, which prepares, with its *alienated universalisation*, the essential conditions for the unfolding of *real universalisation*.

The present work begins from the recognition of the solidary, rational and communitarian nature of human beings, conceived universalistically in space and time. The *Greek world* was the first to highlight this vision, albeit in a non-universalistic, but particularistic way (as it is based on a *narrow* view of man).[57] On its part, the capitalistic cosmos marks, in Hegelian way, the *leaving-itself* of mankind, the alienation from its communitarian essence: it constitutes the negation of the ontological potentialities of man (aurorally encapsulated in Greek thought), his alienation, because it reduces him – in Marcusian terms – to the *one-dimensionality* of the exchange and production of commodities,[58] transforming man himself into a commodity freely circulating on the market and forcing him to think his own present and plan his own future within the only limiting and alienating dimension of the production and exchange of commodities, proclaimed as the only and untranscendible horizon.

It is in the context of this veritative foundation that, in the *Grundrisse*, Marx can establish on the 'free development of individuality' (*freie Entwicklung der*

57 'Narrow' since it does not include women, children, slaves and barbarians.

58 Herbert Marcuse, *One-Dimensional Man. Studies in the Ideology of Advanced Industrial Society* (Boston: Beacon Press, 1964).

Individualitäten),[59] no longer subjugated to the dominion of men and of things, the perspectival nucleus of his *future-centric* phenomenology of the evolution of human history as the realisation of *man's-becoming-man* on a universal scale, in what can legitimately be described as an individualism in search of a new community. This journey towards an Ithaca never reached but ontologically possible is called history. The road that humanity must follow is still long, in order for it to finally reach its *Gattungsmässigkeit* (*conformity to mankind*), realising its own ontological possibilities and giving rise to what Marx already described as the 'development of human abilities as an end-in-itself'.[60]

In the Hegelian philosophical syntax, this translates into a process of development in which the spirit objectifies itself in the world, that is, it becomes other-than-itself, it alienates itself to its complete *self-loss*, to then return to itself enriched by all the determinations attained in this process of self-production and of transition through the *immense power of the negative*. It comprises a process in which mankind 'first becomes estranged from itself and then from this estrangement returns to itself",[61] finally achieving its own ontological potentialities: according to Hegel's formula, 'truth also includes within itself also

59 Marx, *Grundrisse: Foundations of the Critique of Political Economy*, trans. by M. Nicolaus (London: Penguin Books, 1973).

60 'Die menschliche Kraftentwicklung, die sich als Selbstzweck gilt': *DK*.

61 *PG*, p. 36.

the negative', the contradiction, since 'Spirit obtains its truth only when, in its absolute disruption, it finds itself (*gewinnt seine Wahrheit nur, indem er in der absoluten zerissenheit sich selbst findet*)'.[62]

The aim of the present work is to delve into that *immense power of the negative* represented by the dialectical development of capitalism, in the attempt of *looking the 'negative in the face'* and *'dwelling with it'*,[63],[64] so as to decipher it and to identify possible escape routes. In any case, it is necessary to transition through the negative, to know it and to recognise, in Hegelian way, 'the rose in the cross' (*die Rose im Kreuze*),[65] since the real universalisation of freedom coincides with an *Aufhebung* (*sublation*) of negativity itself, and more precisely with the dialectical and immanent overturning of the social totality of absolute-totalitarian capitalism. It comprises an overturning that can only take place within a temporal development of the contradictions structurally present in such a totality. They have reached, in today's globalised world

62 Ibid, p. 32. According to the Hegelian model, subsequently metabolised by Marx, the Christian scheme of the fall followed by redemption, symbolically conceived through that 'vertical' topology structured on the two planes of earth and sky which is at the centre of Dante's *Comedy* (the descent to Hell is the condition for being able to ascend to Heaven), is immanentised in the 'horizontality' of the historical rhythm according to a course that temporally leads to an 'after', which is identified with the overcoming of the fall and with the realisation of mankind.

63 Ibid.

64 Ibid.

65 *GPR*, p. 22.

structure, their highest point of development, configuring themselves as 'so many mines to explode it'.[66]

66 Marx, *Grundrisse: Foundations of the Critique of Political Economy*.

2

HEGEL, THE BOURGEOIS ANTICAPITALIST

'In these opposites and in their complexity, civil society affords a spectacle of extravagance and misery as well as of physical and ethical corruption'.

(Georg W. F. Hegel, *Elements of the Philosophy of Right*)

'History is the journey through which the spirit reveals itself from its initial awareness, still defective and convoluted, and reaches the point where it sees its free self-consciousness'.

(Georg W. F. Hegel, *Lectures on the History of Philosophy*)

There exists a deeply rooted *locus communis*, according to which, the Stuttgart philosopher should be viewed as a *bourgeois* thinker, who, with his own system, did nothing more than to sanctify the capitalistically structured cosmos. It is a common view, which, made possible also by the apparent difficulty of Hegelian terminology,[1] must be destructured not only because Hegel's theoretical greatness leads him, by necessity, to transcend in all aspects his empirical sociological location, but also due to the fact that his own system is innervated by a tension and a dynamism that never merge with the presumed apology of the *status quo* that his name is so often associated to.

In this respect, there is no shortage, in the *ingens silva* of reconstructions, of critical studies that have dwelt on this point, in a number of interpretations that range from those who see in Hegel the features of the progressive reformer, to those who recognise a symbiotic link between *reason and revolution*. Restricting the field to four great

1 In this respect, we must not allow ourselves to be intimidated by the complexity of the Hegelian lexicon. It has been said that the Hegelian system is similar to a carousel which spins fast on itself and on which it is difficult to get on. As long as we stay on the ground, not only is it impossible to decipher its general flow, but we would be even inclined to believe that that motion did not make any sense. However, things would look different if only we are able to get on the ride: then, by participating in the general motion, a wide landscape opens before our eyes, which allows us to re-imagine the initial landscape under a new light. This image forms the basis for the interpretation of Hegel's thought in Jean-Pierre Lefebvre and Pierre Macherey, *Hegel et la Société* (Paris: PUF, 2016). Lukács defined Hegelian thought as a 'democratic gnoseology', because Hegel had conceived it as potentially accessible to all, in a time when Schelling was asserting that only the genius could understand the mystical unity between nature and spirit.

interpretations, which, even in their heterogeneity, are all common to this general scheme, we find *Hegel und die französische Revolution* (1956) by Joachim Ritter,[2] *Der junge Hegel und die Probleme der kapitalistischen Gesellschaft* (1948) by Lukács,[3] *Hegel Secret* (1968) by Jacques D'Hondt,[4] and *Reason and Revolution* (1941) by Marcuse.[5]

2 Joachim Ritter *Hegel and the French Revolution* (Cambridge: MIT Press, 1984) has shown how Hegel's political philosophy may be interpreted in a progressive way: 'there is no other philosophy that, like Hegel's, is also, and even within its innermost impulses, a philosophy of revolution' (Ibid.). Ritter highlights the central role that the French Revolution has exerted on Hegel's intellectual formation, showing how, even after the initial enthusiasm diminished, he never agreed with the Restoration, not even in the Berlin years. Ritter writes: 'the youthful enthusiasm for the present revolution, in Hegel, at the beginning of his philosophical journey, penetrates in his own philosophy and continues to operate in a vital way in throughout his maturity' (Ibid.).

3 Lukács, *The Young Hegel* (London: Merlin, 1975). According to Lukács, Hegel identifies all the main contradictions of the capitalistic cosmos (from alienated labour to exploitation) and elaborates a philosophy that is a real reaction to such a cosmos; in Hegel's anticapitalism will be reread and developed by Marx.

4 Jacques D'Hondt, *Hegel Secret: Recherches sur les Sources Cachées de la Pensée de Hegel* (Paris: PUF, 1968). D'Hondt argues that Hegel is a 'progressive reformer' and points out that all of the repeater-assistants appointed by Hegel were arrested, imprisoned and dismissed as subversives. Moreover, D'Hont shows how Hegel uses an encrypted language in order to circumvent the vigilant censorship, and his whole system is pervaded by an unambiguously Jacobean code.

5 This point has been discussed by Herbert Marcuse, who explained how Hegel's thought, in its every determination, is revolutionary: the rationality of the real must be understood as an ongoing process, not yet completed in the present. In *Reason and Revolution* (1941), Marcuse shows how Hegel conceives *wirklich* not as a dead positivity and the totality of all events, but only as what is 'brought to its concept'.

These four authors have highlighted in various ways how Hegel always adopts an *encrypted language*, in which, behind the mask apologetics of the established order, there exists a *relentless anti-adaptive charge*, the result of the same dialectical movement that sets the pace of the real in its incessant becoming. These interpreters form a single exegetical group from which emerge, as the salient features of Hegelian philosophising, the revolutionary content masked behind conservative language (D'Hondt), the intrinsic expressive function of reason of the revolutionary type (Marcuse), the constant coherence with the anti-adaptive tasks of the French Revolution (Ritter), and the elaboration of philosophical contents destined to prove incompatible with capitalistic society (Lukács).

The anti-adaptive, if not revolutionary character of Hegelian thought, mainly resides in the *expressive function of the anticapitalistic kind* that emerges from his theoretical elaboration, and especially from the fact that with Hegel, as with Fichte, philosophy is conceived as the only adequate tool for reconstituting the social community that has been lost or is in the process of being dissolved.[6] This dissolution is the result of the unleashing of the lethal binomial of the *market* and of the predominance of the *abstract intellect*, which fragments and disjoins all, revealing itself functional to the logics of the destructuring of the Whole and of social

6 Felix Heine, *Freiheit und Totalität. Zum Verhältnis von Philosophie und Wirklichkeit bei Fichte und Hegel* (Bonn: Bouvier, 1980).

atomisation promoted, at the socio-political level, by the Enlightenment movement.[7]

The *reaction to the abstract intellect and to the market* as its essential counterpart takes the form of a return to the veritative space of philosophy, and more precisely to the indivisible unity of knowledge and of the evaluation of the totality of the social being in all its determinations, a unity that stands, in turn, on the rejection of the Kantian *Trennung* (*separation*) between the categories of thought and of being. Hegel's greatness resides, as Fichte's does, in the fact that he does not deplore the Enlightenment with the aim of proposing a return to pre-revolutionary order, following the line of thought that characterises 'the philosophers of reaction' *à la* de Maistre:[8] Enlightenment, for Hegel, represents the dialectical *unity of indispensability and insufficiency*,[9] showing how the positive revolutionary project of world rejuvenation – of which Hegelian thought will never deny the decisive importance at a

7 If Fichte defines his own historical time as the 'age of completed sinfulness', Hegel describes it in terms of a 'transitional gestation time' (*Zeit der Geburt und des Übergangs*, Georg Wilhelm Friedrich Hegel, *PG*), which leads to the establishment of the "animal kingdom of the spirit" (Ibid, p. 535-556), in which personal interest replaces ethical universality and heightens itself as the only universal possible.

8 On the difference between the stance taken by Hegel and nineteenth century Restoration thinkers, see Vincenza Petyx. *I Selvaggi in Europa: la Francia Rivoluzionaria di Maistre e Bonald* (Naples: Bibliopolis, 1988); Petyx, *Dimenticare la Rivoluzione: la Cultura di Destra nella Francia di Fine Ottocento* (Naples: La Città del Sole, 1995).

9 Carla De Pascale (ed.), *Fichte und die Aufklärung* (Hildesheim: Olms, 2004).

weltgeschichtlich (*universal-historical*) level – has instead given rise to a world that is at the mercy of the abstract intellect and of universal selfishness, with the consequence that – as for Fichte – it is necessary to bring such process to completion.[10]

Beyond the wealth of its many variants, the Enlightenment is established, in Hegel's view, on the common theoretical code of anti-communitarian individualism, the foundation of both the supremacy of the abstract intellect and of the autonomisation of the economic sphere in the figure of universal egoism.[11] In order to be able to decipher the essence of Hegel's philosophising, it is necessary to consider that he operates a real *paradigm shift* with respect to the prior juridical-political tradition: if, with the latter, the decisive distinction was between law and morality, with Hegel, it becomes the *separation (ontological and axiological) between the sphere of mere individuals and that of social, ethical and communitarian* entities such as the family, corporations and the state; it represents a separation that, on the one hand, unites what was previously disjointed (morality and law) and, on another, moves further apart what was usually joined, private law (which falls within the sphere of *Recht*) and public law (integral part of the *Sittlichkeit*).

10 Even Jacobean terror is 'necessary and just', if dialectically understood as a part which is in dynamic connection with historical processuality: Hegel, *Jenaer Systementwürfe III*, in *Gesammelte Werke*, VIII, ed. by R. P. Horstmann and J. H. Trede (Hamburg: Meiner, 1976), p. 258.

11 Lewis P. Hinchman, *Hegel's Critique of the Enlightenment* (Gainesville: University Presses of Florida, 1984).

After all, Hegel's irreconcilability with the market system and with utilitarian individualism is strikingly clear if we consider two fundamental aspects of his reflection, briefly mentioned previously: a) the elaboration of a *philosophical science* of totality, into an indivisible unity of method and content, of ontology and axiology, with the obstinate refusal of redefining philosophy as *ancilla scientiae* and, therefore, as an inert mirror-reflection of reality, functional to the mysticism of necessity promoted by capitalism; b) the resolute rejection of the vision of the capitalistic cosmos, which considers the egoistic-economic *civil society* of de-historicised, de-socialised, abstract atoms in agonal competition with each other, as the moral foundation of the world, and the opposition to this by a human community centred on the *Sittlichkeit* and on a sociable and communitarian subject.

Let's start from the first of the themes exposed above. Fichte was the first to highlight, on the one hand, the impossibility of restoring the permanently spent time of the religious-traditional foundation of society and, on the other, the consequent need for the re-establishment of a new social and veritative *fundamentum*:[12] hence, the Fichtean need for the foundation of a *philosophische Wissenschaft* through which truth could finally be reclaimed as a principle and value on which to praxistically plan and implement the redemption of humanity initiated but not yet accomplished by the Revolution. By placing himself at a crossroads between the third (sinfulness) and fourth (redemption)

12 Heine, *Freiheit und Totalität. Zum Verhältnis von Philosophie und Wirklichkeit bei Fichte und Hegel*, p. 46.

age, outlined by the Fichtean *Grundzüge*, Hegel develops, albeit from a different theoretical angle, the Fichtean program of restoring the philosophical science of truth (or of the reestablishment of truth through philosophical science) as the only possible foundation for a new political-social community. If a first definitional approximation is to be attempted, the *Phänomenologie des Geistes* could be labelled as the *reorientation of philosophy in terms of a science*, as a transition from the tension directed at σοφία, towards ascertained and solidly held knowledge, according to the program outlined but not coherently developed by Kant:

> The development of truth in a *systematic science* (*wissenschaftliches System*) can alone be the true shape in which truth exists. To help to bring philosophy nearer to the *form of science* (*Form der Wissenschaft*), so that it may reach the goal where it can lay aside the name of *love of knowledge* (*Liebe zum Wissen*) and be *actual knowledge* (*wirkliches Wissen*), is what I have set before me.[13]

The *Vorrede* of the *Phänomenologie* is filled with such formulations, which express the necessity by philosophy to attain the statute of unshakable knowledge without, for this reason, risking the neutralisation of its veritative space: 'the true figure of truth is therefore placed in scientificity (*die wahre Gestalt der Wahrheit in die Wissenschaftlichkeit*

13 *PG*, p. 5.

gesetzt wird), and this is the same as saying that truth finds the element of its existence only in the *Concept*'.[14] Hegel connects this scientific requirement of philosophy with the fundamental traits of his time, consistent not only with the definition of philosophy envisaged in the *Grundlinien* (*ihre Zeit in Gedanken erfaßt, its time apprehended in thoughts*),[15] but also with the *real scission* undertaken by the *Aufklärung* which, historically, constitutes the 'source of the need for philosophy'.[16] It is the world born out of the French Revolution, with its lethal union of Robinsonian individualism (Marx's 'Robinsonades') and empirical utilitarianism, to raise the prospect of a philosophical reconstitution of the fabric of society, overcoming the divisions that the new world has generated.

Only the present age, the age of toil *par excellence*, having turned its back on the past, is able to find a way of *exposing* (*darstellen*) philosophical truth, so that philosophy may

14 Ibid, p. 24: 'It is only as a system that knowledge is actual and can be presented as science' (*das Wissen nur als Wissenschaft oder als System wirklich ist und dargestellt werden kann*). It is Hegel himself to enunciate the identity of 'phenomenology of spirit' as the anti-development and reformulation of *Philosophie* as *Wissenschaft* (Ibid, p. 27): 'this phenomenology of Spirit presents the becoming of science in general, that is, of knowledge' (*dies Werden der Wissenschaft überhaupt, oder des Wissens*). Hegel then goes on to say (Ibid): 'In order to become genuine knowledge, or to produce the element of science that is the pure concept of science itself, immediate knowledge must travel down a long and arduous path'.

15 *GPR*, p. 23.

16 Hegel, 'Differenz des Fichteschen und Schellingschen Systems der Philosophie (1801)', in *Suhrkamp-Werkausgabe* 2 (Frankfurt: Suhrkamp, 1979), p. 20.

attain the more solid statute of *Wissenschaft*,[17] since – in coherence with the presupposition that 'the negative is also positive' – [18] negativity in its most radical form must be understood as the necessary transition so that its overcoming can lead to the reconstitution of the preceding social synthesis at a higher level. Only the present time can then reveal itself as being 'ripe for *the elevation of philosophy to science* (*die Erhebung der Philosophie zur Wissenschaft*)'.[19]

The Hegelian concept of *Darstellung* requires further consideration. The term is employed, in the *Vorrede* of the *Phänomenologie*, in the sense of a *self-development* that presents the structure of Totality and that, for this very reason, is composed of the unity between the *telos* and the entire journey undertaken to reach it: indeed, philosophical truth implies the *becoming-of-itself*, in that circular form which requires the temporal mediation of development and which only at the end of the process can be said to have acquired its full expression.[20] We are therefore in the presence of a temporal development that sets the pace of the process by which the Spirit fully comes

17 It is easy to agree with Habermas when he identifies in Hegel 'the first philosopher who developed a clear concept of modernity': Habermas, *The Philosophical Discourse of Modernity*. Hegel is the first thinker to have thematised modernity and its self-ascertainment as *Grundfrage*. And even if Hegel was not the first philosopher of the modern world, or the first philosopher who reflected on aspects of modernity, he is undoubtedly the first for whom 'modernity has become a problem'.

18 *WL*, p. 369.

19 *PG*, p. 5.

20 Ibid. p. 19.

to itself after having transitioned through the *ungeheure Macht des Negativen*: in opposition to any irenic and naively linear conception, in Hegel's polemological perspective, development is intertwined with positions, mediations, oppositions and conflicts that enable, between regresses and setbacks, a progressive advancement towards the Absoluteness of Spirit, which is no other than the very beginning of the story, but which acquires its actual reality only at the end of the process (*das Wahre ist das Ganze*). The truth of the process therefore rests in its fulfilment, that is, in the final result, since 'only in the end it is what it is in truth'.[21]

Thus, Totality is given as 'the movement of the positing of itself' (*die Bewegung des Sich-selbst-setzens*),[22] which is 'mediation between the becoming-other-than-itself and itself'.[23] The Spirit, as conceived by Hegel, is the process of a Subject that has within itself *reference* and *determinateness* and that is itself, as Spirit, only if 'in its being outside of itself, remains within itself',[24] in a dialectical process of self-development in which alienation and disalienation constitute two essential poles in dialectical correlation. As an appropriate method for expressing the Spirit, the *Darstellung* addressed by the *Phänomenologie* thus coincides with that movement which Hegel defines as *mediation* (*Vermittlung*) and which is characterised

21 Ibid, p. 20.

22 Ibid.

23 'Vermittlung des Sich-anders-werdens mit sich selbst': Ibid, p. 18.

24 Ibid.

as a *becoming-other* of a subject that reaffirms itself, subsequently, as a *self*, but at a higher degree: 'the *living substance* (*lebendige Substanz*) constitutes the being that is truly *subject*, that is truly real, only insofar as it is the movement of the positing-itself, only insofar as it is a mediation between the becoming-other-than-itself and itself'.[25]

These passages centred on the notion of *Darstellung* can be integrated with others taken from the *Wissenschaft der Logik* and instead based on the *Vorstellung*. The contradiction is 'the root of all movement and vitality',[26] with the consequence that 'real movement [...] is no other than the notion that something is, in itself, self and the lack of self (the negative of itself), in one and the same respect'.[27] In similar fashion, the *becoming-other* (*Veränderung*), which is at the same time *contradiction* and *movement*, is present 'in every reality as well as in every concept'.[28] What distinguishes speculative thought – the *philosophische Wissenschaft* – from the simple *Vorstellung* is the way in which they relate to the contradiction.[29] While the former has the courage of *looking the power of the negative in the face*, and to heroically reside within it, the *Vorstellung* is unaware of the contradiction,[30] even though it also finds

25 Ibid.

26 *WL*, p. 382.

27 Ibid.

28 Ibid.

29 Volker Ruhle, *Verwandlung der Metaphysik. Zur systematischen Darstellung des Absoluten bei Hegel* (München: Fink, 1989).

30 Malcolm Clark, *Logic and System. A Study of the Transition from "Vorstellung" to Thought in the Philosophy of Hegel* (Hague:

itself immersed in it, because it finds itself entangled in the empirical particular while rejecting the observation of the whole in its dynamic and conflictual development:

> *Something is therefore vital only insofar as it contains within itself the contradiction* (*Etwas ist also lebendig, nur insofern es den Widerspruch in sich enthält*) and it is this very force of understanding and sustaining the contradiction in itself. [...] *Speculative thought consists only in this, in holding firm the contradiction* (*das spekulative Denken besteht nur darin, daß das Denken den Widerspruch und in ihm sich selbst festhält*) and holds itself in the contradiction, but not in a way, as for the *representation* (*Vorstellung*), that it would allow itself to be ruled by contradiction, and this to dissolve all its determinations into other determinations or into nothing.[31]

In no lesser measure than the *Darstellung*, the *Vorstellung* is ensnared in the contradiction, but it is unaware of this, it is not conscious of the contradiction that it *has* and that itself *is*: '*therefore representation has contradiction everywhere for content but fails to become conscious of it* (*das Vorstellen hat daher wohl allenthalben den Widerspruch zu seinem Inhalte, kommt aber nicht zum Bewußtseyn desselben*)'.[32] The *Vorstellung* is, by its nature,

Nijhoff, 1971).

31 *WL*, p. 383.

32 Ibid, p. 384.

only *incomplete mediation*, insofar as *true* mediation is a *passage*, thus the arriving at one end coming from another, but it also involves *self-removal*. The *Vorstellung* presents itself as an *incomplete mediation* precisely because it lacks the necessary force to exercise the negation, the moment of the antithesis: inextricably tied to the contradiction that it is but that it is unable to see, it cannot operate the *true mediation* and, therefore, retains an open scission between *thought* and *sensible matter*, arresting in the moment of the *abstrakter Verstand* and of the scission of the parts from the whole.

On their part, the Spirit and its *Darstellung* are able to go beyond the contradiction, precisely because they are aware of it: they are innervated by the movement and by the dynamics of *becoming-other*, then finding themselves again, because they see the *becoming-other* as the physiognomy of a moment internal to the Spirit itself, that is, they conceive the contradiction as a moment of the whole, as a necessary part of the whole and of its dynamics of development. Only the *Darstellung* of the *philosophische Wissenschaft*, assuming as its object of analysis the totality in its dynamic and processual determinations, can understand the contradiction of the immense power of the negative inherent to the time of *gestation and transition* generated by the Revolution.

After all, only in this way, by recognising the contradictions with respect to the whole, can we understand the progressive dialectical attainment of self-consciousness by humanity in its process of emancipation and of universalisation of freedom, which constitutes the immanent narrative of historical becoming, in its movement of *becoming-other-than-itself* to then *return-to-itself* enriched by the transition through the negative.[33] The Spirit's finding itself again is then its knowing itself as Spirit, as the subject of a Totality that is *self-movement* and that, *eo ipso*, gains experience of *becoming-other*, of the contradiction, but that at the same time negates the other as *independent*, it neutralises it by recognising it as a moment of totality (*negative* if considered in itself, *positive* if located in the processual dynamics of which it constitutes only a transitory moment) and finding itself again in the absolute fragmentation.

History thus becomes the gradual development by which the rationalisation of the real unravels – according to the dynamic identity of *wirklich* and *vernünftig*[34] – through the locating and overcoming of contradictions, in that *reconciliation* (*Versöhnung*) which is only possible in the Odyssean form of a *return to the self* after being *lost* and having become *strangers to the self*, by self-alienation: this is the history of human consciousness outlined in the *Phänomenologie*, in accordance to which freedom is a historical attainment in the *formative novel* of humanity, whose *Gestaltungen* are metaphors of as many *educational* moments of awareness of individuals as well as of mankind.

33 The Spirit becomes one with itself, through an activity that negates and, at the same time, incorporates the 'other-than-itself'.

34 *GPR*.

Alongside the worldly religious model of fall and redemption,[35] the source of inspiration for this conception still remains the Fichtean perspective of the development of the entire human culture as the result of an *original self-positing* (and not of divine emanation),[36] in a process in which the *negative* is a necessary obstacle that must be historically produced to then be overcome, generating the advancement and unfolding of emancipation.[37]

If we now turn to the second of the two aspects that we proposed to investigate, namely the explicit Hegelian rejection of the capitalistic cosmos, we must reflect on both themes of the *Sittlichkeit* and of the critique of *social atomism* of the *system of needs* of the *bürgerliche Gesellschaft*. The connection with the problem of the *Darstellung* of the *philosophische Wissenshaft* is evident. In the *Rechtsphilosophie*, of the three sections dedicated to *civil society* (*bürgerliche Gesellschaft*), the first deals with the needs and antagonisms of civil society abandoned to itself,[38] while the second and third deal with the juridical

35 Hermann Krings, *Die Entfremdung zwischen Schelling und Hegel: 1801-1807* (München: Bayerische Akademie der Wissenschaft,1977).

36 William Hartkopf, 'Die Dialektik Fichtes als Vorstufe zu Hegels Dialektik', *Zeitschrift für philosophische Forschung*, 21.2 (1967), 173-207.

37 Giuseppe Vasta, *Storicità e Metastoricità dell'Alienazione nella Fenomenologia dello Spirito di G.W. Hegel* (Palermo: ILA, 1987); Günter Rohtmoser, *Théologie e Aliénation dans la Pensée du Jeune Hegel* (Paris: Beauchesne, 1970); Peter Cornehl, *Die Zukunft der Versöhnung: Eschatologie und Emanzipation in der Aufklärung, bei Hegel und in der Hegelschen Schule* (Göttingen: Vandenhoeck & Ruprecht, 1971).

38 With regard to the traditional Marxist confusion on Hegel's

relations regulated in it through the action of the ethical force of the State,[39] which brings order to the chaos of the economic system. As the realm of the economic and earthly gains of the autonomisation of the economy promoted by liberal thought, *civil society* is outlined by Hegel,[40] on the one hand, as the place of individual uprooted subjectivities, bent on themselves and monadically *without windows* (Leibniz), and on the other, as the utilitarian nexus that is established between these *in-dividuals* by virtue of the market as the space of contractual bargaining and of relations aimed at achieving personal gain.[41] Utilitarianism, in the sense of a metaphysical *envelope* enshrouding *homo oeconomicus*, generates that network of autonomous individualities held together by the *universal egoism* that Fichte had already identified as the true cause of the age of sinfulness: '*the egoistic purpose* (*der selbstsüchtige Zweck*) – writes Hegel in paragraph 183 of the *Grundlinien* – conditioned in this way by *universality* (*Allgemeinheit*), establishes a *system of omnilateral dependence* (*System allseitiger Abhängigkeit*)'.[42] The *Vorstellung* promoted by the abstract intellect, the residing in the contradiction

concept of civil society, see: Umberto Cerroni, *Societa Civile e Stato Politico in Hegel* (Bari: De Donato, 1974).

39 On the hegemonic role of the State in Hegel, see: Franz Rosenzweig, *Hegel und der Staat* (Berlin: Suhrkamp, 2010).

40 *GPR*; and Ian Fraser, *Hegel and Marx. The Concept of Need* (Edinburgh: Edinburgh University Press, 1998).

41 Margery Rosinger, *Die Einheit von Ethik und Ontologie bei Hegel* (Frankfurt: Lang, 1980); Robert B. Pippin and Otfried Höffe, *Hegel on Ethics and Politics* (Cambridge: Cambridge University Press, 2004).

42 *GPR*, p. 221.

without identifying it, is the very form of the illuministic conception and of its rejection of the dimension of processual totality, with the consequent autonomisation of the *abstract* negative moment with respect to the process of which it is part.

Compared to the *particular altruism* of the family – the first moment of *Sittlichkeit* –,[43] which is an immediate and natural union of the sexes for the procreation and breeding of the offspring, civil society corresponds, in Hegel's view, to the kingdom of *universal egoism*, configuring itself as *System der Bedürfnisse* established on the antagonism of individuals each aiming at their own individual gain. From this egoistic determination emerges the web that connects *civil society*, the hendiadys of *abstrakter Verstand* and *Vorstellung*:[44] as the product of the *intellect*, which fragments reality, showing its single portions one independent of the other, civil society is the realm of the self-interest of those who see the parts but not the whole that accommodates them, without being able in this way to decipher with the philosophical *Dartstellung* the contradiction that shrouds the *bürgerliche Gesellschaft*, that place in which 'the *particularity for self* (*Besonderheit für sich*), as an omnilateral fulfilment of one's needs, of contingent

43 On Hegel's concept of the family, see: Rudolf J. Siebert, *Hegel's Concept of Marriage and Family. The Origin of Subjective Freedom* (New York: Edwin Mellen Press, 1998).

44 Umberto Curi (ed.), *Società Civile e Stato fra Hegel e Marx* (Padova: CLESP, 1980).

arbitrariness and of subjective caprice, in its enjoyment, destroys itself and its own substantial Concept'.[45] Indeed, in the *bürgerliche Gesellschaft*, the representations of the abstract intellect promote, on the one hand, the delegitimisation of the knowledge of totality and, on the other, the interest of the empirical particular against the universal, with the consequence that it becomes possible to assert that 'in civil society, the Idea is lost in particularity',[46] in the atomistic plurality of the unrelated and irreducibly conflicting parts. The result is a shattered social world, to which social inequality and class division are coessential, a realm in which 'disproportionate riches' are concentrated in a few hands:[47] 'in these oppositions and in their complicated relations, civil society also offers the spectacle of debauchery, of misery and of physical and ethical corruption which are common to both sides'.[48]

It is within this theoretical context that the *Hegelian critique of English political economy* may be identified as a science of the *abstrakter Verstand*, as can be found midway through paragraph 189 of the *Grundlinien*. In one way, Hegel praises the new economic science, which has allowed a deeper understanding of society compared to the explicative models traditionally proposed by morality and by religion;[49] in another, however, he does not forget his

45 *GPR*, p. 222.

46 Ibid, p. 259.

47 Ibid, p. 266.

48 Ibid, p. 222.

49 Christopher J. Arthur, 'Hegel on Political Economy' in *Hegel and Modern Philosophy*, ed. by David Lamb (London: Croom Helm, 1987), pp. 102-118.

fundamental critical evaluation, by which the economic approach of political economy remains the partial and not concrete approach of the *Vorstellung* of the abstract intellect that does not know how to think the empirical particular in dynamic connection with the universal. It is able to explain the genesis of the modern *system of needs*, which however – contrary to the claims made by political economy – does not coincide completely with the *objektiver Geist*, with the historical objectification of society as a whole:

> *Political economy* (*Staatsökonomie*) is one of the sciences that, originating in the modern age, have found their most suitable element in it. Its development shows the interesting spectacle of how thought (see Smith, Say, Ricardo), beginning from the infinite multitude of particular facts with which it is initially confronted, extracts the simple principles of the Thing and resolves the activity of the *intellect* (*Verstand*) that controls the Thing. To recognise, in the sphere of needs, this manifestation of Rationality that is inherent and active in the Thing, on the one hand, has a conciliatory effect, but on the other, this manifestation is indeed the field in which the intellect, with its subjective purposes and its moral opinions, vents its own discontent and its *moral peevishness* (*moralische Verdrießlichkeit*).[50]

50 *GPR*, p. 227.

It is on the same critique of the intellect's abstract particularism that Hegel, in paragraph 198 of the *Grundlinien*, identifies, in the *division of labour* (*Teilung der Arbeiten*),[51] the essence of the *Abstraktion* implemented by the modern economic system, in which the logic of dislocation and fragmentation is brought to its extreme consequences in the form of the assignment to each worker of a single, monotonous and alienating operation to be carried out for the entire working day, according to a theme also developed in the *Enzyklopädie* (§§ 525 -526).[52]

Predating the *Frankfurter Schule* authors by more than a century,[53] Hegel unmasks, in the pages of his

51 Ibid, p. 232.

52 'In this particularity of needs the glimmer of universality is found in the way the intellect creates differences in them, and thus causes an indefinite multiplication both of needs and of means for their different phases. Both are thus rendered *increasingly abstract* (*immer abstrakter*). This differentiation of content by abstraction gives rise to the *division of labour* (*Teilung der Arbeit*)': EPW, § 525. 'The labour which thus becomes more abstract tends on one hand by its *uniformity* (*Einförmigkeit*), to make labour easier and to increase production — on the other hand, to limit each person to a single kind of technical skill, and thus produce *more unconditional dependence on the social system* (*zur unbedingtern Abhängigkeit von dem gesellschaftlichen Zusammenhange*). Skill itself becomes in this way mechanical, and acquires the capability of letting the machine take the place of human labour': Ibid, § 526.

53 Theodor W. Adorno and Max Horkheimer, *Dialectic of Enlightenment* (New York: Verso, 2016): the main thesis of the book is, as is known, describes the overturning of Enlightenment into its opposite (it should have emancipated and instead it generated extermination camps, it should have produced science and instead it turned into myth), and therefore into the 'self-destruction of Enlightenment'. The result is the gloomy concentrationary landscape in which 'humanity, instead of entering a truly humane state, sinks into a new kind of barbarism', revealing in this way the

Phänomenologie, the *dialectical dynamics* of the Enlightenment, its inversion into the fideistic cult of reason and of empirical datum, into the blind *fury of the vanishing* (*Furie des Verschwindens*),[54] and into the absolutism of the abstract intellect.[55] After all, the Stuttgart philosopher points out that the atheism praised by the *philosophes* is profoundly ambiguous: it does not correspond to the mere assertion of the non-existence of God, but it rather configures itself as the loss of interest for truth and, at the same time, as the irrational faith in the omnipotence of the intellect.[56] To this *loss of interest functional to the dominance of profit*, Hegel does not react by reaffirming truth in the old religious form, nor by denying it in the new form – which is essentially the same but in opposite form – of Enlightenment: on the contrary, he furnishes it with a *new philosophical foundation*, reaffirming on new grounds the veritative character of philosophical knowledge as the science of the whole.[57]

The world of civil society, autonomised by the Enlightenment, corresponds to a return to *sense-certainty* promoted as the only possible truth: in this way,

truth of Enlightenment: 'Enlightenment is totalitarian'. See also Arnold Künzli, *Aufklärung und Dialektik: politische Philosophie von Hobbes bis Adorno* (Freiburg: Rombach, 1971).

54 *PG*, p. 589.

55 D'Hondt (ed.), *Hegel et le siècle des Lumières* (Paris: Presses universitaires de France, 1974).

56 Fabrizio Sciacca, *Imago Libertatis. Diritto e Stato nella filosofia dello spirito di Hegel* (Turin: Giappichelli, 1996); Lino Rizzi, *Eticità e Stato in Hegel* (Milan: Mursia, 1993).

57 Claudio Cesa, *Stato e Libertà negli Scritti Politici di Hegel* (Florence: Olschki, 1971).

consciousness 'now returns to this reality after having completed the transition through its own experience',[58] and 'this new sense-certainty is no longer *opinion* (*Meinung*), but rather *absolute truth* (*absolute Wahrheit*)',[59] which cannot be subjected to discussion nor to criticisms. Thus, the illuministic rationalism is overturned, dialectically, into intolerant faith and into the sacralisation of the factual datum. It is in this reconversion of philosophical truth into certainty of the intellect that the *hegemony of the useful* can fully unfold – 'everything is *useful* (*nützlich*)'[60] – since, if released from the whole that accommodates it, 'every part is so much in-itself as for-another',[61] and, for this very reason, is regarded true *insofar as it is useful*. The truth of the parts fragmented by the intellect resides in their *usability*, in coherence with the algid laws of the *mos oeconomicus* of the calculating *Verstand*. Man himself loses his autonomous value and becomes a *thing among things*, so much important as he is useful: 'as everything is useful to man, so too man acquires the trait of utility, and his determination is therefore to become a *universally useful* (*gemeinnützlich*) and usable member of the troop'.[62] The veiled accusation that Hegel makes against empiricist and utilitarian England, by claiming the impossibility, for a people, of being civil without a metaphysics is, for this reason, a critique of the device of the market's fetishistic

58 *PG*, p. 791.
59 Ibid.
60 Ibid.
61 Ibid.
62 Ibid, p. 560.

autonomy and of the delegitimisation of philosophical knowledge.[63]

Through its main commandment – 'things are purely and simply useful, and must be valued only on the basis of their utility',[64] – the Enlightenment is overturned into *spiritual animal kingdom* (*geistiges Tierreich*),[65] into that universal *reification* under the sign of commodities that Hegel cleverly encapsulates, in the *Phänomenologie*, with the formula *the thing is I* (*das Ding ist Ich*).[66] The outcome is precisely that commercial anarchy critically outlined by Fichte, against which the only possible antidote is offered by the destructuring of the atomistic-egoistic subject and by the revival of the hegemony of the polity as the basis for a new solidary community:[67]

> Against the regulation from above by public arrangements, therefore, particular interest invokes the freedom of trade and commerce; but the more blindly it immerses itself in its egoistic ends, the

63 Norbert Waszek, *The Scottish Enlightenment and Hegel's Account of Civil Society* (Dordrech: Kluwer, 1988); David MacGregor, *Hegel, Marx and the English State* (Boulder: Westview, 1992).

64 *PG*, p. 791.

65 Ibid, p. 536.

66 *PG*, p. 791.

67 See M. Cacciari and U. Curi, 'L'intelletto Scientifico come Radice 'Animale' del Politico in Hegel', in Wanda Tommasi, *La Natura e la Macchina. Hegel sull'Economia e le Scienze* (Naples: Liguori, 1979); and Mario Tronti, *Hegel Politico* (Rome: Istituto dell'Enciclopedia Italiana 1975); Jean-Louis Vieillard-Baron, *Hegel, Penseur du Politique* (Paris: Le Félin, 2006); Bernard Bourgeois, *La Pensée Politique de Hegel* (Paris: PUF, 1969).

> more it requires such regulation to bring it back to the universal, to mitigate those dangerous and sudden convulsions and to shorten the duration of time in which its *collisions* (*Kollisionen*) have to reconcile on the way of an *unconscious need* (*bewusstlose Notwendigkeit*).[68]

Hegel's *unhappy consciousness* resides in his explicit formulation of the need to abandon the *Besonderheit* of the system of needs, and therefore his particular sociological position that would induce him to supinely accept the utilitarian order, in order to adhere to the *real universal*, the inversion of the *bürgerliche Gesellschaft*'s universalised egoism – and therefore particularism. The particular to which Hegel should empirically adhere – society that elects profit to an absolute criterion – is identified in its contradictory character by speculative reason, which contextualises it in the dialectical movement of Totality and which, *eo ipso*, deciphers its status of mere negativity functional to the unfolding of universal freedom of which that moment is the negation and, at the same time, the necessary precondition.[69]

In the same way that the adherence to the *Sittlichkeit* against the *Moralität* implies the development of a communitarian and historically determined subject, the recognition of the *Staat* as a higher ethical realisation with respect to the *bürgerliche Gesellschaft* equally entails

68 *GPR*, p. 262.

69 Axel Honneth, *Leiden an Unbestimmtheit: Eine Reaktualisierung der Hegelschen Rechtsphilosophie* (Stuttgart: Reclam, 2001).

the hegemony of the political aspect over the economic one. If it is true that, beginning from the *Fragmente über Volksreligion und Christentum* (1794),[70] the private sphere of social atoms is always identified with the negative moment, whereas the public sphere of ethical community constitutes the positive one, it is also true that only with the codification of the State as the supreme moment of ethicality and of social synthesis, is it able find its highest expression in the principle of the *primacy of the real human community* over the false universality of the universal egoism, typical of the atomistic aggregation held together by an *unsocial sociability*. In the *ethical totality* (*sittliche Einigkeit*) the whole comes before the parts ('by nature a people comes before the individual'),[71] and it is superior to them: hence, the attack that Hegel moves against the theoreticians of the *social contract*, due to the fact that the latter is no other than a surreptitious transposition of an institution concerning private law into the superior sphere of public law,[72] 'into the absolute majesty of ethical totality'.[73] The mistake made by *contractualists* is twofold, because they conceive the superior public sphere according to the parameters of the private one,[74] and, at the same time, by

70 Hegel, *Fragmente über Volksreligion und Christentum*, 1794;

71 Hegel, *Über die wissenschaflichen Behandlungsarten des Naturrechts*, ed. by G. Lasson, vol. VII, p. 371.

72 For a discussion on the problem of the contract in modern political philosophy, see Patrick Riley, *Will and Political Legitimacy. A Critical Exposition of Social Contract Theory in Hobbes, Locke, Rousseau, Kant, and Hegel* (Jan Jose: ToExcel, 1999).

73 Hegel, *Über die wissenschaflichen Behandlungsarten des Naturrechts*, cit., p. 405.

74 'The aggregate of private persons is often spoken of as a people:

following the dictates of the abstract intellect, they see the abstract-formal individual as a logical and chronological *prius* with respect to communitarian ethicality, theoretically opening the way to utilitarian individualism.[75]

Bobbio raises an important point when he affirms that 'Hegel's philosophy of right was, of the school of natural right, not only the dissolution but also, in a sense, its fulfilment',[76] because, in one way, it fully rejects the categories with which natural law elaborates its own theory of State (the concept of state of nature, of social contract, of voluntary association, etc.), dismissing them through the atomistic individualism on which they are founded, and in another, it *makes truthful*, by establishing it on new foundations, the absolute rationality of the State with respect to the unruliness of pre-State societies: the rational truth of the State no longer coincides with the truth of reckoning typical of the Hobbesian abstract intellect, but with the objective reason that is crystallised in historical institutions and that sets the rhythm for the temporal process of the universal unfolding of freedom.

After all, not only does Hegel oppose the dislocating movement that, along the downhill path which leads to present-day neoliberalism, aims at the neutralisation

but as such an aggregate it is *vulgus*, not *populus*: and in this respect it is the only aim of the State that a people should not come to existence, to power and action, as such an aggregate': *EPW*, § 544.

75 On Hegel and natural law, see Jean-Louis Vieillard-Baron and Yves Charles Zarka (ed.), *Hegel et le Droit Naturel Moderne* (Paris: Vrin, 2006).

76 Norberto Bobbio, *Studi Hegeliani* (Turin: Einaudi, 1982), p. 175.

of the State in favour of the *system of needs*, but it also finally corrects the tendency of classical natural law, which identified in the State a moment in itself functional to the atomistic character of individualities. With Hegel, the rationality of the State is in fact directly linked to the communitarian aspect of *ethical life*, which is pre-eminent with respect to the individual. In this perspective, the Stuttgart philosopher never aims his critique at the concept of individual freedom, but rather at the dual movement of its absolutisation and neutralisation of the superior moment of the freedom of ethical community ('nothing has become more ordinary than the idea that each should limit his own freedom in relation to the freedom of others').[77],[78]

The structurally anticapitalistic expressivity of Hegel's system thus primarily emerges from the universalistic communitarianism in which it is embedded.[79] It comprises a *universalism of emancipation*, because it is centred on the view of history as the theatre of the immanent dynamics of universal liberation.[80] The Hegelian position is indeed innervated, in all its articulations, by the communitaristic-

77 On Hegel's criticisms of the liberal conception of freedom, see Steven B. Smith, *Hegel's Critique of Liberalism: Rights in Context* (Chicago: University of Chicago Press, 1989); Alan Patten, *Hegel's Idea of Freedom* (Oxford: Oxford University Press, 1999), pp. 82-103.

78 *EPW*, § 539; on the communitarian and non-individualistic aspect of knowledge in Hegel, see Terry Pinkard, *Hegel's Phenomenology. The Sociality of Reason* (Cambridge: Cambridge University Press, 1994).

79 Preve, *Hegel Antiutilitarista* (Rome: Settimo Sigillo, 2007), p. 40.

80 Ibid, p. 9.

universalistic duality:[81] it is *communitaristic*, insofar as it refuses to thematise ethics deprived of its concrete historical-communitarian dimension (hence the scathing attack against the *Sollen* of the *schöne Seele* inherent to the Kantian *Moralität* of the single, abstract and de-historicised subject), and *universalistic*, as it proposes a rationalistic model of progressive universalisation of behaviours and of freedom. The two Kantian aspects of *Sollen* and of *moral of intentions* are rejected by Hegel as products of the *abstrakter Verstand*, as they presuppose their carrier to be an abstract and formal subject, who is eradicated from his communitarian *ethos*.[82]

If the abstract intellect finds its own privileged political sphere in autonomised civil society, then philosophical reason, in turn, addresses the ethical totality of communitarian life. Functional to a historical, communitarian, political and *naturaliter* heteronomous subject, the *Sittlichkeit* is 'the Idea of freedom as the living Good' (*die Idee der Freiheit, als das lebendige Gute*),[83] that

81 Ibid, p. 13-14.

82 Furthermore, these aspects end up producing the two essentially correlated outcomes of the *frustration* of the subject, who may never fully correspond to the concept of 'duty', and of the *justification of evil* when it derives from good intentions (the inversion of Jacobean virtue in the terror of the guillotine). Even the most catastrophic outcomes of my action can then be justified.

83 *GPR*, § 142. The real object of political thought is the *Sittlichkeit*, 'ethicality', 'social ethics'. *Sittlich* is he who behaves according to the ways and customs of the socio-political sphere in which he lives: the *Sittlichkeit* includes the three inseparable terms of 'custom' (*Brauch*), 'habit' (*Gewohnheit*) and 'conduct' (*Benehmen*). Social ethics does in no way coincide with political economy, nor can it be deducted from the sum of social atoms formed from the abstract

is, the set of social customs that form the indispensable connective fabric of every human community.[84] This latter is reconceived and re-established by Hegel on new, rational, universalistic and dialectical grounds, with a complete and explicit parting from the old foundations (this explains, furthermore, the Hegelian extraneousness to the party of the old classes that, in Prussia, supported Metternich).

Incompatible both with the *abstract subject* of the *formalistic* line, and with the *homo oeconomicus* produced in the image and likeness of utilitarianism, but also with the *disjointed subject* which develops along the theoretical axis that stretches from Hume to Nietzsche, the Hegelian ethical subject – the direct heir of the Aristotelian ζῷον πολιτικὸν –[85] finds its own supreme realisation in the *Sitten*

notion of *homo oeconomicus*. See Manuela Alessio, *Azione ed Eticità in Hegel. Saggio sulla 'Filosofia del Diritto'* (Milan: Guerini, 1996).

84 Lukács' *Zerstörung der Vernunft* – certainly a questionable text by many respects – highlights an essential point, which enables to reconsider Adorno's ungenerous view, according to which the only reason to be 'destroyed' by Lukács' text would be that of its author: the diatribe that sees Hegel and Schelling in opposition is not only a more or less civil academic clash between two different theoretical profiles, but is rather an actual *Kampfplatz* between the construction of dialectics as the framework of a new ethical world, removed from the anarchy of the market, and the flight towards irrationalism and the consequent acceptance of the illogical logic of the new structure of the world. Schelling may *not* be regarded as an idealist *tout court*, because after his initial adherence to Fichte's idealism and after the subsequent identity of nature and spirit, he quickly emerges from the idealistic path to arrive at a different way of philosophising. Lukács, *The Destruction of Reason*, trans. by P. R. Palmer (London: Merlin, 1980).

85 Joachim Ritter, *Metaphysik und Politik. Studien zu Aristoteles und Hegel* (Frankfurt: Suhrkamp, 1969).

of his community and he 'is therefore in relation with ethical powers as he is with what is substantial, with duties which are binding by his own will'.[86] In this way, freedom does not coincide with an abstract *ought-to-be*, individually pursued, but on the contrary it is a *given world* (*vorhandene Welt*),[87] a consolidated range of traditions historically determined in one's community.[88]

The State itself – with its *universal altruism* – becomes the place of fulfilment and of full realisation of the *Sittlichkeit*, since it projects on a universal scale the particular altruism of the family mediated by the negative of the universal egoism of the *bürgerliche Gesellschaft*.[89] In virtue of the

86 *GPR*, § 148.

87 Ibid, § 142. After all, this perfectly accommodates Hegel's critique to Rousseau's 'fury of the vanishing', the contractualist error by which, in order to be able to establish the new egalitarian (and individualistic: abstract community of uprooted and primary individuals, not deduced from the customs of the pre-existing community) social contract, it is necessary to 'skip' all intermediate moments (the family, the professional corporation) to immediately reach Emile's community and the *New Heloise*.

88 With respect to these, the individual realises himself as a free communitarian individual, inseparable from the communitarian 'substance' to which he belongs. '*In an ethical community* (*in einem sittlichen Gemeinwesen*), it is easy to say what someone must do and what the duties are which he has to fulfil in order to be virtuous. He must simply do what is prescribed, expressly stated, and known to him within his situation': Ibid, § 150. 'The ethical as *ethos*, appears as custom and the habit of the ethical appears as a *second nature* (*zweite Natur*) which takes the place of the original and purely natural will and is the all-pervading soul, significance, and actuality of individual existence. It is *the Spirit living and given as a world* (*der als eine Welt lebendige und vorhandene Geist*), and only thus does the Substance of spirit begin to exist as Spirit': Ibid, § 151.

89 Claudia Mancina, *Differenze nell'Eticità: Amore, Famiglia, Società Civile in Hegel* (Naples: Guida, 1991).

hegemony of the political dimension characterising it, the State neutralises the disjoining forces of the anarchy of the market and guarantees full and stable existence to the community. As Hegel states, 'the State is the reality of the ethical idea' (*der Staat ist die Wirklichkeit der sittlichen Idee*),[90] 'ethical Spirit as substantial will' (*der sittliche Geist, als der substantielle Wille*),[91] and 'the Rational in-itself and for-itself' (*das an und für sich Vernünftige*).[92],[93] It is not a case of the *objektiver Geist* subordinating the market to the State, but rather the economic sphere to a *superior moment of social synthesis*, advancing an economy that is *embedded* in the social fabric of the ethical world, against the inversion operated by utilitarianism through the hegemony of civil society over the State:

> If the State is confused with civil society, and if its specific end is placed in the security and protection of property and of personal freedom, then the interest of individuals as such becomes *the ultimate purpose* (*der letze Zweck*) of their unity and, at the same time, the fact of being a

90 *GPR*, § 257.

91 Ibid.

92 Ibid.

93 Alien to the 'totalitarian' logics that have been attributed to it by different twentieth century scholars, the Hegelian State is a political organisation that concretely accomplishes the main achievements of the French Revolution, as is after all attested by the semantic value of the concept of *Staat* in the years of Hegel's writings. See Reinhart Koselleck *et al.*, 'Staat und Souveranität', in *Geschichtliche Grundbegriffe*, VI (Stuttgart: Klett-Cotta, 2004), p. 1-154.

member of the State becomes a matter of individual caprice.'[94]

In the symbiotic relation – already formulated by Fichte – of development of the individual and of the community, a truly human universalisation then becomes possible, one that is not only the market-driven caricature that universalises only the commodity form, conforming all human beings to the single reified model of producer and consumer.

94 *GPR*, § 257.

3

FURY OF THE VANISHING. THE ANNIHILATION OF BOURGEOIS ETHICALITY

> 'The human individual is not an atom. Immanent to the concept of individual is the concept of society.'
>
> (Giovanni Gentile, *Genesis and Structure of Society*)

Absolute capitalism is, by its nature, hostile towards any form of ethical, professional, sentimental, and existential stability. It fulfils the premises that, with the *Communist Manifesto* of 1848, Marx and Engels already identified as the foundations of its logic of development.

Far from being a conservative system and opposed to innovation, as often is erroneously believed, the capitalistic mode of production presents an intrinsic vocational passion for change and instability. It lives in the incessant Heraclitean transformation of the world which it forged in its own image.

Unlike the previous forms of production and of social relations, which were essentially established on the preservation of given conditions and on the 'unchanged preservation of the old structure of production',[1] capital always exists by revolutionising, without respite, the means of production and the social relations in which it is structured, making this relentless change its very foundation. The total mobilisation of the existent is its inevitable basis.

These prerogatives may be attributed to what Pasolini already defined as 'revolutionary, progressive and unifying neocapitalism',[2] which transforms all in the name of progress, unifying the entire world under the sign of fetishised economy. It lives by making liquid and iridescent what, in previous forms of production, was given in stable and rigid forms, if not completely ossified:

> The constant upheaval of production, the incessant questioning of all social conditions, the perpetual uncertainty and

1 Karl Marx and Friedrich Engels, *The Communist Manifesto* (London: Penguin Classics, 2014).

2 Pier Paolo Pasolini, *Saggi sulla Politica e la Società* (Milan: Mondadori 2016), p. 861.

motion, separate the bourgeois age from all those that preceded it.[3]

This tendency, inscribed in the premises and promises of capital ever since its very inception, may be said to have reached its completion with the transition into the absolute phase, corresponding to the time of global flexibility and of universal transiency. All that is solid melts into air and has become liquid.[4] The logic of the precarious system of needs is now based on the flexibilisation of life, on the destabilisation of what is stable, and on the liquefaction of the solid: there is no stable foundation that can resist. Following Habermas' formula,[5] capital is a 'completed project', fully realised in the real and symbolic immanence of production and of exchange.

The precarisation of the real and symbolic spheres is one of the founding premises and promises of the capitalistic power relation, today having reached the full correspondence *in actu* with its own concept through the task of universal transiency of flexible accumulation. The increase in the rates and intensification of production and circulation of commodities, which emerges from the programmed obsolescence dictated by trends, reveal how the virtual basis of capitalism and the concrete basis of its absolute form is that very *creative destruction*, the *zerstörende Aufbau der Welt* evoked by Kafka, which, as the

3 Marx and Engels, *The Communist Manifesto*.

4 Marshall Berman, *All That is Solid Melts Into Air. The Experience of Modernity* (New York: Simon and Schuster, 1982).

5 Habermas, 'Die Moderne: ein unvollendetes Projekt' in *Kleine politische Schriften (I-IV)* (Frankfurt: Suhrkamp, 1980), p. 444.

real fury of the vanishing that dissolves all, also evaporates every solid reality. Here lies the intimately nihilistic essence of capital and of its *cupio dissolvi*.

Consistent with the logic that marks the transition from the dialectical to the absolute phase, even with the aspects of stability and solidity, there is a tension arising between the bourgeois and capitalistic elements; a tension that is resolved with the annihilation of the bourgeois element in the transition into the absolute, de-ethicised and anti-bourgeois system of needs. The bourgeoisie, which is also a hegemonic class in the dialectical phase, forges its own world centred on stable values, and on what, with Hegel, we could legitimately define as the *Sittlichkeit*, the *ethicality* founded on *ethical roots*, on the monogamous family and on classical education, on the State as the guarantor of the community and of the primacy of the political over the economy, of the social over the private, of rights over competitiveness.

Capitalism, in its evolutionary dialectics, which are exclusively oriented to the nihilistic unlimited expansion of the commodity form and to the infinite valorisation of value, finally devastates that world with which it too had hitherto coexisted. The bourgeois ethicality, centred on the value of stability and on solid forms, cannot subsist in the framework of absolute chrematistics. Its two founding concepts are incompatible with the absolute post-bourgeois and post-proletarian market system: namely, ethicality *a)* is based on stability and on rootedness, on the solid planning of life in relation to married life, social status, active citizenship, culture, which cannot be incorporated in the framework of a flexible capitalism centred on the logic of *short-terminism* and *precarism*; b) then, establishes itself on the communitarian and solidary forms of existence and, even from this point of view, it is irreconcilable with the post-bourgeois and ultra-capitalistic dynamics of the individualistic privatisation of society, of the mercantile corporatisation of existences, and of the commercialisation of politics and of life. With Schmitt's syntax, the capitalistic historical world that is still permeated by not yet fully commodified values, transitions 'into the general economisation of spiritual life and into a structure of the spirit that finds the central categories of human existence in production and consumption'.[6]

The family community, the community of civil society guarded by ethical roots, the national state community with its primacy of the political over the economy, comprise realities that, because of their stability and their communitarian value, must be crushed by absolute capitalism: which aims, for this reason, to de-ethicise itself, disjoining every stabilised and solidary communitarian connection, to then recompose them according to the logic of that market-driven unsociable sociability which gives rise to the competitive society built on non-social foundations. The latter exists in the form of a de-ethicised civil society, which would be more appropriate to define as a *system of needs*, with its sociable unsociability, cosmopolitanism, youthism and liberal-libertarianism.

6 Carl Schmitt, *The Concept of the Political* (Chicago: Chicago University Press, 2008).

The dissolution of the solidary bonds and solid identities inherent to communitarian ethicality appears as a fundamental moment for the redefinition of de-ethicised individualities into competitive atoms of consumption, into entrepreneurs of the self and into commodities that must valorise themselves by placing themselves in circulation on the smooth surface of the market without frontiers and without any ethical limitations.

If the community is, by its very nature, the dynamic space of a relation of recognition between equally free and solidary individuals, then a fundamental moment of the absolutisation of capital is its nullification in the name of the redefinition of society, in terms of an atomistic system, made to measure for monads that have no windows other than those of the unsociable sociability of the free-exchange system.

As we shall see, the absolute chrematistic system can justly be described, with Hegel's categories, as the system of planetary needs freed from any residual moments of ethicality (from the family community to the State, from public institutions to *ethical roots*).

This generates a form of society that is not communitarian, and that is established on the dependence between competitive atoms and on what Kant at the time of his *Idea for a Universal History with a Cosmopolitan Purpose* (1784) defined as the *ungesellige Geselligkeit*, or the *unsociable sociability*:

> By antagonism here I mean the unsociable sociability of men, that is to say their tendency to unite in society, which is however tied to a continuous resistance that continually threatens to dissolve this society. Human nature bears the evidence of all this. Man has an inclination to associate: since, in this state, he feels in greater measure himself as a man, thus he feels the development of his own natural dispositions. But he also has a strong tendency to isolate himself: because he also finds in himself the unsociable property of wanting to conduct everything according to his own interests, and therefore he expects resistance from all sides, in the same way that he knows of himself that he, in turn, is inclined. to create resistance to all others.[7]

The State represents the fulfilment of *ethical life* (*sittliches Leben*), since it stands as the guarantor of the stability of the community. It politically controls and regulates the economy, avoiding its absolutisation, and allows each singularity to fully develop within the framework of the communitarian ethicality of which it is part. It makes possible, through its work, 'the equal dignity and independence' of men and citizens.[8] Moreover

7 Immanuel Kant, 'Idea for a Universal History from a Cosmopolitan Point of View (1784)' in *On History*, trans. by Lewis White Beck (New Jersey: Prentice Hall, 2001).

8 Hegel, *Werke in zwanzig Bänden* (Stuttgart: Frommann 1969-1979), XX, 22, p. 7.

– even after Hegel – it promotes communitarian ethicality through specific institutions such as marriage and school, social security and university, the pensions system and the protection of the vulnerable. It prevents the Master from taking control in an absolute form and from dissolving the ethical community.

In the *bürgerliche Gesellschaft*, in the *civil society* in its lowest moment, that is, the one of the unsociable sociability of the egoistic system of needs, what prevails is that acquisitive individualism, which, as Gramsci pointed out, becomes *animal-like apoliticism*.[9] The representations of the abstract intellect promote the interest of the empirical particular against the universal, with the consequence that it is possible, according to Hegel, to assert that 'in civil society, the Idea has lost itself in the particularity',[10] in the atomistic plurality of the unrelated and irreducibly conflicting parts.

The result is a fragmented social world, to which social inequality and class division are consubstantial; a realm in which 'disproportionate riches' are concentrated in a few hands,[11] and the community is dissolved under the unregulated, competitive and individualistic pressure of the *spiritual animals* of the economy. Hegel writes:

> With these oppositions and their intricate relation, civil society also offers the

9 Antonio Gramsci, *Prison Notebooks* (New York: Columbia University Press, 2011).

10 *GPR*, § 229.

11 Ibid, § 244.

> spectacle of debauchery, misery, and physical and ethical corruption common to both sides.[12]

Hence the need, inevitable in Hegel's view, of a politicisation of the economy, so that the State can control it and prevent the production of the *tragedies in the ethical* (*Tragödie im Sittlichen*) caused by the rapacious egoism that dissolves the community in the name of egoistic individualism. The solidary and ethicised community must prevail over the egoistic, privatistic and individualistic drives of the unsociably sociable system of needs.

With its ethical roots permeating civil society, the State consolidates the moment of the universal, preventing the supremacy of egoistic particularism. It prevents society from dissolving into the individualistic acquisitive egoism that, following the tradition first initiated by Locke and then by Smith, would comprise the only adhesive for an abstract coexistence of unsociably sociable monads.

To Hegel, civil society, far from being a market in which mutually indifferent individuals negotiate with each other according to the practices of the *do ut des*, instead configures itself as a universal family and, consequently, as a solidary relation between members of a community having imprescriptible rights which are themselves material, that is, filled with content. In this perspective, the ethicality thematised by Hegel presupposes and incorporates the natural rights of traditional natural-law inherent to man *qua talis*: however, they cease to be moral presuppositions

12 Ibid, § 238.

and become state institutions, realised in the concrete *ethos*, thus retaining their universality. Through the institutions of the State, politics can guarantee the stability of ethical roots and, therefore, the safekeeping of the community as a society whose members recognise themselves as parts of the totality and who actively pursue its interest.

For the first time, with Hegel – who celebrates all the revolutions that constellate modernity and who considers the monarch simply as a sort of dot on the 'i' – inalienability does not refer to nature, but to universal history: which has gained, over time, indispensable acquisitions, constituting a patrimony for man. Hegel's philosophy considers legitimate the modern age and, at the same time, the process of emancipation that has developed from it to be not yet fulfilled.

The very fact that, in Hegel's view, the first fundamental right is *the right to life* (*das Recht zu leben*), becomes the basis for the redefinition of the relation between politics and economy, in the sense of a rational control of the latter by the former; a control made possible by the actions of the State and the concrete ethical roots permeating civil society.

Even from this perspective, there is an abyssal distance separating Hegel from the liberal tradition and, moreover, from the neoliberalism that is coessential to the absolute market system of de-ethicised market society.

If the liberal tradition tends to know only negative rights

and conceives freedom itself in a negative form (as 'freedom from'), in Hegel's view there are *materielle Rechte, material rights* filled with concrete contents which the ethical power of the State must guarantee for each individual as a member of the universal family of civil society. Thus writes Hegel, in open opposition to the liberal tradition:

> Everyone has *the right to live* (*das Recht zu leben*) and this right must not reside solely in defence. He has not only this negative right, but also a positive right. The reality of freedom is the ultimate purpose of civil society. The fact that man has the right to live implies that he has a positive, filled right. The reality of freedom must be essential.[13]

It is clear that in this passage Hegel is targeting Locke and his followers, guilty of having conceived freedom as a simple absence of interference by the State or as an active intervention by the latter to guarantee the property of individuals: in the words of Locke's *Treatise on Government*, which condenses the conception of the liberals, 'the preservation of property is the purpose of government and the reason for which men enter society' (II, § 138). Society itself, according to the model inaugurated by Hobbes' Leviathan, is conceived in a non-social and programmatically anti-communitarian way as an aggregation of antagonistic and competing individualities, who enter in relation with each other driven exclusively by

13 Ibid, § 118 A.

their own individual interest and by the will to maximise the effects of their own acquisitive egoism.

With a complete inversion of a perspective that was common to Plato and Aristotle in antiquity, and subsequently, albeit on different grounds, to Hegel, for Hobbes, Locke and the liberal tradition, the community is not the logical and chronological *prius*, the reality that enables the genesis and the development of free individualities. On the contrary, it is a derived and secondary moment, the result of the union of already formed and autonomous individualities, who unite in a secondary moment not because they are intrinsically sociable and communitarian, according to the Aristotelian perspective, but because they are aware that their acquisitive egoism can find a freer and more effective realisation only in the context of a competitive intersubjective relation, with respect to which State power is called to perform the exclusive function of night watchman and of *pouvoir neutre*.

According to Wilhelm Röpke, the ordoliberalist founder of *social market economy*, the State should limit itself to 'oversee with absolute impartiality and incorruptibility for the most strict observance of the rules of the game and of sporting correctness'.[14] Justice would only be found in this. To this thesis, we could object, not without good reason, that it is difficult to define as just a situation in which the slaughter of the weak occurs without the active

14 Wilhelm Röpke, *The Social Crisis of our Time* (London: Transaction Publishers, 2009).

intervention of those who, in theory, could and should do so. On the other hand, justice would coincide with the ethical intervention of a State that would normalise the relationship by preventing the strongest from slaughtering the weak.

4

COMMUNITARIAN ETHICALITY AND ACQUISITIVE INDIVIDUALISM

> 'Against nature no one can claim a right, but in the condition of society a defect immediately acquires the form of injustice'.
>
> (Georg W. F. Hegel, *Elements of the Philosophy of Right*)

If, with Hegel, the individual is the origin and not the community (to be understood, on the contrary, as an aggregation of independent individualities each operating for their own interest), it follows that, for the liberal perspective, the community makes sense insofar as it guarantees the independent development of the individual according to competitive and antagonistic logics inherent to the system of needs. Consequently, the State is called upon to enforce only the formal rights protecting the free intersubjective transactions between competitive atoms that relate to each other on the exclusive basis of the logic of free-exchange, centred on personal profit and acquisition.

From being a social relation characterising the community as a place of free, ethical and solidary individualities, freedom is thus redefined as the possibility by the sovereign individual, owner of property, to protect his own particular economic interest undisturbed, without interference by the State and by the community redefined as a system of competitive atomistics.

Fichte, in the pages of *The Closed Commercial State*, had already overturned Locke's perspective, focusing his attention on those material rights which, he believed, the liberal tradition forgets: 'the task of the State is first and foremost to give each one his own, placing him in his property, and then protecting him'.[1] With no less passion, even Hegel is opposed to the merely negative freedom advocated by the liberals. The State must not simply guarantee that the individual serenely benefits from his possessions. It must also ensure that there is no individual who is deprived of basic material rights, whatever his social condition. As Fichte had already explained, it goes against reason 'that one can buy the superfluous, while any one of

1 Johann Gottlieb Fichte, *Sämmtliche Werke*, III (Berlin: De Gruyter, 1965), p. 399.

his fellow citizens lacks the necessary and cannot afford to pay for it'.[2]

From this perspective, it becomes apparent why the two *grand récits* feeding the dominant narrative should collapse. The first is the one according to which the State is, as such, an enemy of individual freedom, which only the liberal tradition can guarantee. In the Hegelian ethical system, on the other hand, the State's ethical power stands as a guarantee for the equal freedom – formal and material – of every citizen, member of the universal family of civil society. Certainly, there can be frictions and conflicts between family ethics and State ethics, as the tale of Antigone reminds us: but this does not prevent, in general terms, the main task of the ethical roots of civil society ethicised by the State, consisting in the continuation – and not in the opposition – of the effort undertaken within the family. Instead, it is the liberal tradition that contradictorily tends, on the one hand, to promote the overcoming of the State as a form that limits the self-regulating free game of the economy and, on the other, to conceive the State in a repressive and authoritarian form, as *minimal State* and *night watchman* which, as such, stands as the armed guard of the dominant classes and certainly not as a communitarian ethical power. Paradigmatic of this is the fierce and ruthless repression that for a long time in Western societies has been carried out against workers' associations, guilty of violating the liberal principle of individual trading.

2 Ibid, p. 409.

The second great narrative that the Hegelian ethical system undermines, concerns the presumed realisation of free individualities as the exclusive prerogative of the liberal tradition. From the Hegelian point of view, liberalism *à la* Locke tends to deny the individual in the very act with which it would like to free him. Indeed, it moves from the assumption that, in general, the freedom of the politically unregulated market generates balance and well-being, knowing that for some citizens the outcomes will be quite the opposite.

Liberal freedom intended in a merely negative form as *freedom from* and, therefore, as a license for the strong to massacre the weak, then, poses itself as a force to annihilate the development of free individualities: it denies some material rights to some individuals, because there is no ethical power to guarantee them politically. Consequently, only the ethical power of the State can guarantee the free development of communitarian individualities:

> It is said that, in general, the balance always restores itself: this is correct. But here we are dealing with the particular no less than with the general. Therefore, this must be resolved not only in a general manner, but it is individuals as particularities to constitute a purpose and to have rights.[3]

Hegel is here suggesting that the market could even restore its own balance: but this will occur in general terms,

3 Hegel, *Vorlesungen über Rechtsphilosophie 1818-1831*, ed. by K.-H. Ilting (Stuttgart: Frommann, 1973-1974), III, p. 699.

at the cost of individuals, who will fall into misery and lose everything. Therefore, Hegel believes that the market may not be abandoned to itself: it must be politically disciplined, governed and regulated, so that 'individuals as particularities' may constitute an end in themselves in a stable manner, and have rights regardless of the laws of market economy.

Only with the active intervention of politics through the ethical power of the State is it possible to guarantee that each individual, as a member of the community intended as a universal family, permanently enjoys the fundamental (material and formal) rights conferred upon him as a heir of the communitarian organism:

> The ultimate end is the particular individual; it is necessary to provide for individuals and no one must rely on the principle that things will fix themselves.[4]

As paradoxical as it may seem in a time, like the present, infected by the omnipervasive rhetorics that celebrate the dithyrambic song of the free individual guaranteed by the Stateless market, it is only the political power of the State that can fully protect the free individuality that each member of the community represents: indeed, only the State can protect him from the tragedies in the ethical of the economy abandoned to itself; which, even with its balance restored, would not cease to throw into misery many members of the less well-to-do classes.

4 Ibid.

Indeed, to the ethical State, individuals are not competitors called upon to individualistically protect their particular interests in the context of the *bellum omnium contra omnes* of the market economy. On the contrary, they are members of the universal family of the community and, as such, regardless of the different social positions, they are bearers of equal rights and equal duties.

For this reason, Hegel thinks that there can be concrete circumstances in which 'the right to property can and must be violated'.[5] This is, for example, the case of those who are dying of hunger: he has the right to steal, 'has the right to such illegal action'.[6] More precisely, in this case it is not even, strictly speaking, a violation of rights, but the affirmation of a higher right, that to life. Thus writes Hegel:

> The man who is dying of hunger has the absolute right to violate the property of another; he violates the property of another only in a limited way. The right of *extreme need* (*Notrecht*) means that it does not violate the right of the other as a right: the interest is directed at this piece of bread; he does not treat the other as a person without rights.[7]

The opposition to the liberal tradition and to its neoliberalist deviation is strikingly obvious. If to Locke and to today's captains of market theology the questioning

5 Ibid, p. 157.

6 Ibid, p. 402.

7 Ibid, p. 341.

of private property is violence and a violation of rights, in Hegel's view, on the other hand, violence and a violation of rights is to absolutise it at the expense of the political community and of solidarity in favour of privatistic property over the communitarian one.

Prior to Marx, Hegel already knew that inequality also neutralises freedom and that, consequently, the alternative – so dear to the liberal tradition – of equality and freedom, is an abstraction devoid of any content: there may be freedom only in a community of equally free individuals, being equality, according to Hegel, the condition in which 'the other must not be in a position of advantage with respect to my existence'.[8]

Equality, therefore, does not coincide with equal formal freedom (which could, indeed, coexist – and in capitalism it does – with the greatest economic inequality), but comprises equal material freedom, that is, the assurance, for every member of the universal family of the community, of a sphere of rights that are inaccessible to the *lex oeconomica* and permanently guaranteed by the ethical power of the state.

In the absence of equality, there can be no freedom. For this reason, the widespread extreme poverty, where the economy is depoliticised and detracts from the control of the State, 'invests the entire extension of the realisation of freedom',[9] and turns into the 'total lack of rights'.[10] In

8 *GPR*, § 63 A.

9 Hegel, *Vorlesungen über Rechtsphilosophie*, IV, p. 342.

10 *GPR*, § 127.

the context of an ethical State with an economy that is politically governed and functional to the community, the pauper – Hegel explains – can instead appeal to a right that corresponds to an 'obligation of civil society'.[11] The fury of economic increase and of competitiveness is, to Hegel, only restrained and limited by the ethicising power of the State and by the primacy of the political that it guarantees.

For this reason, in the de-ethicised, absolute, flexible and post-1989 system of needs, the globalist Master aspires to the integral de-politicisation of the economy and, in a converging manner, to the destructuring of the State as a power able to limit it and to discipline it in view of the common good of the *Gemeinschaft*, the ethical-solidary *community*: 'against the superior regulation by public power – Hegel says – particular interest precisely invokes the freedom of the industry and of commerce',[12] of competitiveness and of the absence of State and political ties. In this way, what prevails is the freedom coessential to the capitalistic mode of production, thus, with Fichte's formula, the freedom 'of making one another fall into ruin'.[13]

In the horizon of classist society, the *freedom* of some to accumulate limitless riches, coexists with the *freedom* of others to starve to death. Deprived of any connection with the social community, freedom is degraded to a private business for individuals without a community and to free

11 Hegel, *Vorlesungen über Rechtsphilosophie*, IV, p. 604.

12 *GPR*, § 237.

13 Fichte, *Sämmtliche Werke*, III, p. 457.

competitive entrepreneurship. Furthermore, freedom is understood and practiced only as the individualistic liberalisation of customs and of consumption and, therefore, as the liberation of the sphere of circulation from what is still forbidden by the persistence of religious, ethical and political ties. In Schmitt's words: 'liberalism is a doctrine of freedom, freedom of economic production, freedom of the market, and above all, the queen of all economic freedoms: freedom to consume'.[14]

The only allowed freedom in the monocultural horizon of the politically correct *pensée unique* is that coinciding with liberalism, that is, with the self-government of the wealthy global classes which, with the symbolic mediation of the intellectuals as the dominated part of the dominant class, demonise every alternative conception of freedom and of social and economic organisation as totalitarian. Furthermore, the only democracy tolerated and glorified in the realm of global chrematistics is that coinciding with the plebiscite of private capital markets and of the liquid and unrestricted finance of Wall Street and of The City.

More precisely, the non-democratic democracy that capital produces in its own image – the *free market democracy* – is, *de facto*, the order of limitless financial capitalism, of the universalism of rights of consumerist freedom for post-identitarian and abstract individuals, who are in a state of perpetual Brownian motion on the frictionless and multi-directional plane of the global market. In the context of the new re-feudalised order,

14 Schmitt, *The Concept of the Political*.

the authority is no longer emanated from the political sovereignty inscribed in the spaces of national States, but from money, which is sovereignless, immaterial money and free from any legal, political or ethical conditioning.

The newspeak of the *pensée unique* calls it *democracy*, when in reality the new globalised society presents itself as an ironclad oligarchy of billionaires of the stateless upper class of New York and San Francisco, electorally endorsed by a plebeian class composed of dimidiated citizens (and redefined as consumers), deprived equally of the informative base necessary for a correct analysis of media manipulation, and of the fundamental rights – still guaranteed in the context of bourgeois and proletarian capitalism – for an existence worthy of free people.

According to the dominant ideology, there is full correspondence between democracy, freedom and capitalism: therefore, anyone who criticises the latter is unreservedly exorcised also as an enemy of the first two. For this reason, the neoliberalist de-ethicisation involves the destruction of the State as the culminating moment of bourgeois ethical life, so that the de-politicised economy may become the only sovereign reality and, equally, that the ethical bonds of the community may be dissolved, themselves regarded incompatible with the dynamics of limitless expansion of the commodity form in every direction. In this new context, the neofeudal Lord may dominate unchallenged.

Therefore, the integral de-ethicisation marks an inevitable passage for the realisation of absolute and flexible capitalism, the foundation of which is given by destabilisation, mobilisation and eradication. Instability and precarity, in their absolute and total forms, triumph in the time of dissolved ethicality, in the Hegelian sense, and of the evaporated father, in the Lacanian sense (*l'évaporation du père*), that is, where the Law has been annihilated and life is no longer regulated by fixed rules.

5

HEGEL AND THE PRIMACY OF ETHICAL LIFE

> 'Each of us has the aim to intuit *himself* in the other'.
>
> (Georg W. F. Hegel, *Philosophy of Spirit, Jena Lectures*)

In the present globalised age, the liquid and unlimited flow of financial capital, which moves unhindered across the world reduced to smooth and fluid plane, requires as its inevitable condition the dissolution of every solid element, both at the real and symbolic levels: at *the real level*, by the demolition of national State borders, the destruction of every state not part of the single market (hence the rhetoric of the *rogue States*, of the ethical imperialism of human rights, of *new Hitlers* as pretexts for new Hiroshimas etc.), the complete de-politicisation of the economy, the removal of any sovereignty on a global scale; at *the symbolic level*, through the destructuring of values and of the symbolic sphere not yet intrinsic to capital, but then also through the complete de-ethicisation of the world of life, or rather the destruction of the ethical element not yet completely incorporated into the logics of omni-commodification.

The fact that, together with the fetishistic absolutisation of the commodity form and of the *bad infinite* (Hegel) of the valorisation of value, everything must be entrusted to universal competitiveness and to the laws of the market, necessarily implies the neutralisation of the bourgeois Superego, but then also the dissolution of all that is able to form an opposition, because of its stability and extraneousness to the logics of exchange value, the precarious rhythm of *the new way of the world* .

For this reason, the fully reified present cannot accept and, instead, must promptly remove both Hegel's and Marx's profiles, not only because they educate to dialectical reason, and therefore, to think beings in their becoming (against the dogma of *capitalismus sive natura* and of the *end of history*), and to identify the contradiction as the engine of historical totality.

Moreover, the globalistic system of production and exchange aims, on the one hand, to expunge every residual element of Hegelian bourgeois ethicality (the State, the family, the welfare system, the primacy of the political, religion, formative education, etc.), so that the post-bourgeois and ultra-capitalistic order inherent to the absolute phase may affirm itself without restrictions. And, on the other, it aspires to remove, with Marx, every revolutionary yearning, every anti-adaptive utopia and every spirit of scission aimed at achieving human emancipation and the transcendence of the fully alienated present.

From a different perspective, the post-bourgeois chrematistic system assumes as its own teleological orientation the annihilation both of the ethical element incompatible with omni-commodification (Hegel), and the utopian-conflictual element of the unhappy consciousness in search of an ennobling and mobilising ulteriority (Marx). It destroys in equal measure the ethicality and unhappy consciousness of the bourgeoisie, as well as the struggles and the *dream of something* (Marx, see letter to Arnold Ruge) of the proletariat. And, with impeccable coherence, it condemns Hegel and Marx as *enemies of the open society*, according to the Popperian formula, which has today become the explicit model of financial aristocracy (*Open Society Foundations* was, by no coincidence, the name chosen by the stateless Lord of competitivism George Soros, for his organisation).

The new way of the world must, indeed, favour an anti-bourgeois, anti-proletarian and ultra-capitalistic structure, without the return of any red flame able to reignite the spirit of utopia. In order for absolute and post-bourgeois capitalism to be instituted, it must undertake the complete disintegration of all the elements of bourgeois ethical life, from the family to job stability, from solid communitarian relations to education as the formation of men with roots and possessing cultural depth.

In other terms, there must be a complete production of precarity of the real and symbolic spheres, so that the de-socialised, de-stabilised, de-ethicised individual, magnified to autocratic atom and, analogously to Leibniz's monads, physiologically *without windows*, is abandoned, in his solitude, to the power of the new monotheistic *lord of the world*, the sovereign market.

The individual, deprived of any social bond, must also not have any cultural depth nor an identity capable of inducing him to contest the total falsehood which he is inhabiting. In the age of the death of God, of the death of the Ideal and of the social bond, the individual can abstractly achieve anything, and concretely nothing (or rather, he is free only insofar as he is a consumer). In the very moment in which he is magnified by the neoliberal rhetorics as sovereign of himself and of his world, he becomes completely subjected to the world of things and of flexible production.

In the words of Adorno: 'the state of things in which the individual disappears is also that of unbridled individualism, in which *anything is possible*'.[1] In this resides the paradox highlighted by Adorno of a society which has legitimised itself on the basis of the sovereign and free expansion of individuals and which is today accomplished with their complete annihilation on the altar of the absolute market.

1 Theodor W. Adorno, *Minima Moralia. Reflections on a Damaged Life*, trans. by E. F. N. Jephcott (London: Verso, 2005), p. 149.

Unlike traditional communitarian structures, the market that has today occupied God's vacant place does not favour the establishment of stable identities and of a strong self. Instead, it must destructure them, so that the self remains permanently precarious and unstable, manipulable and unable to say no, and is therefore shaped by the forces and offers of the market, as well as by the flow of information managed by the *industry of consent*.[2]

The Heraclitean circulation of commodities redefines human subjectivity in unstable and precarious forms, unconditionally open to all solicitations and stimuli. It neutralises any residual capacity of dispersed identities for contesting and, therefore, for resisting consumeristic pressures. In the absolute phase, the subject, reduced to hedonistic atom of mindless and potentially unlimited *jouissance*, is finally devoid of critical spirit and personality, alleviated of any symbolic relation that is not the code of the commodity form.

As shown by Hegel in his 1821 *Elements of the Philosophy of Right*, the foundation of bourgeois ethical life may be legitimately recognised in the stability or, if one prefers, in the temporal consolidation of guaranteed forms of the existential, affective and working life. In particular, as the culminating moment of the *objective Spirit*, for Hegel, ethicality is the highest level of overcoming and truth-becoming of the synthesis of the *abstract right* (*abstraktes Recht*), or the moment of

2 Alain de Benoist, 'On Identity', *Telos* 128 (2004), 9-64.

pure and abstract external formality, and of *morality* (*Moralität*), or the law of individualised interiority.

The *Sittlichkeit* incorporates the universal exteriority of the abstract right. On the other hand, it preserves the feeling of adherence by the individual's consciousness as an aspect of morality.[3] By opposing himself to abstract individualism and to the fragmentation promoted by the Enlightenment and the abstract intellect, Hegel firmly believes in the necessity of the re-establishment of the solidary community as the foundation of social and political life.

For Hegel, the Enlightenment is indispensable and, at the same time, insufficient: indispensable, because it has dissolved the order of the *ancien régime*; insufficient, because it has abandoned society, dissolved into the nomadic plurality of the competitive individualities connected only by the unsociable sociability of the system of needs, better redefined as the system of atomistics.

For this reason, in Hegel's view, it makes no sense to regret the past of feudal society devoid of individual recognition, nor to remain at the disrupted and atomised society promoted by the disjoining logic of Enlightenment. Instead, it is necessary to pursue the creation of new communitarian syntheses able to recompose the whole, at a higher level, from its fragmented and ossified abstract parts: in Ilting's words, 'Hegel believes that in his time it is necessary to re-establish the ideas of the community, of

3 Allen W. Wood, *Hegel's Ethical Thought* (Cambridge: Cambridge University Press, 1990).

solidarity and of the social responsibility of citizens as the basis of social and political life'.[4] From the period ranging between 1798 and 1799, and not without idealisations, Hegel laments the 'nostalgia for the lost life',[5] for the 'beautiful ethicality' of the ancient world. However, this is not a languid and passive nostalgia but an operative one, setting itself the task of recovering what is lost and of establishing a community that is superior even to the previous one.[6]

Indeed, for Hegel, the community is not a reality already established in customs and traditions, it is instead a dimension that must be constituted through the active participation of individuals. As highlighted by D'Hondt, Hegel's political thought, centred on the figure of communitarian and solidary ethicality, is oriented 'by rejecting the return to the feudal past, exposing the defeats and weaknesses of liberalism'.[7]

With ethicality, *concrete freedom* unfolds in the form of the realisation of personal singularities in the interest of the universal which they perceive as their own substantial spirit in communitarian ethical life:

> Concrete freedom consists in the fact that personal singularity and its particular

4 Karl-Heinz Ilting, *Aufsätze über Hegel* (Frankfurt: Humanities Online, 2006).

5 Hegel, *Theologische Jugendschriften*, ed. by Herman Nohl (Frankfurt: Minerva, 1996) (henceforth abbreviated to *JS*), p. 282.

6 Zbigniew Pełczyński, *Hegel's Political Philosophy. Problems and Perspectives* (Cambridge: Cambridge University Press, 1971).

7 D'Hondt, 'Hegel e il Socialismo Nascente', in *Rivista di Filosofia*, 1977, p. 93.

> interests, in one way, have their complete development, and the recognition of their right, to themselves (in the system of the family and of civil society); and in another, they partly pass from themselves into the interest of the universal (*Interesse des Allgemeinen*), and partly, with their knowledge and will, they recognise the universal itself: more precisely, they recognise it as their own *substantial Spirit* (*substantieller Geist*), and they are active in view of it as if in view of their ultimate purpose.[8]

Therefore, Hegelian ethicality may rightfully be regarded as a non-coercive form of public ethics, but exercised freely by individuals as binding. They fully recognise themselves in the solidary and communitarian relations that make them feel as integral parts of the *ethos* of a people, and in which they can fully realise themselves as social individuals. Subjectivity is realised in the form of a personal particularity attached to the substantial unity of communitarian life:

> The principle of modern States has this immense strength and depth: it enables the *principle of subjectivity* (*das Prinzip der Subjektivität*) to be fulfilled to the autonomous extreme of *personal particularity* (*persönliche Besonderheit*), and, at the same time, it repositions it

8 *GPR*, § 260.

> within the *substantial unity* (*substantielle Einheit*), thus preserving the latter in that very same principle.[9]

In the sphere of ethicality, the individual 'is therefore in relation with ethical powers as he is with what is to him substantial, with obligations which are binding by his will'.[10] He does not perceive them as foreign and coactive, as instead is the case for *abstract right*, but as his own very essence, as the concrete and communitarian implementation of his own potentialities.

In the context of ethicality, with the transition to civil society, the original unity of the family as an immediate natural community founded on feelings is lost. Such unity must, therefore, be recomposed by overcoming the scission and, for the same reason, taken to a higher level: from immediately and originally given (the family), it must be posited through mediation to overcome the scission (the State). Here is what Hegel writes regarding the scission resulting from the transition from the family to the system of needs:

> The moments bound to the unity of the family, since the family is the ethical idea still in its concept, must be released from the concept to an autonomous reality – this is the stage of difference.[11]

9 Ibid.

10 Ibid, § 148.

11 Hegel, 'Grundlinien der Philosophie des Rechts', *Vorlesungen über Rechtsphilosophie*, II, § 181, p. 628.

What emerges from this passage is that the logic of the *'in-itself'*, of the *'out-of-itself'* and of the *'in-itself and for-itself'* also characterises the sphere of the world of ethicality: indeed, the family is the ethical community in-itself, originally a given, and crystallised in the natural immediacy of feelings.

Instead, civil society, especially in the figure of the system of needs, corresponds to the transition out-of-itself, or to the loss in the fragmentation, to the objective dispersion and to the sociably unsociable relation between competitive atoms, where, dissolved in the atomistic system, the ethical community must find and reconstitute itself through effort and in mediated form. As Hegel points out: 'the spirit is higher than nature',[12] which is *ein verborgener Geist*, 'a hidden spirit' or, more precisely, the spirit that represents itself as something other than itself: nothing is contained other than in the spirit, the spirit itself being as other than itself, a spirit that is temporalised and, therefore, spatialised, becoming, in fact, nature. Nature is 'boring history with the same course',[13] whereas the spirit is 'the changing manifestation that the spirit gives of itself in ever different forms'.[14] Similarly, the system of needs is the ethicality that has negated and *concealed* itself, representing itself as other than itself, as de-ethicised system. The immediate ethics of the

12 Hegel, *Über die wissenschaftlichen Behandlungsarten des Naturrechts*, ed. by G. Lasson, VII, p. 464.

13 Hegel, *Vorlesungen über die Philosophie der Geschichte* (Frankfurt: Suhrkamp, 1970), p. 56.

14 Ibid.

family must be reconquered as the mediated ethics of the State.

Indeed, the State represents the fulfillment, in- and for-itself, of the *reality of the ethical idea*, the realisation of an ethicality that knows of itself and wants itself as the whole and as its parts: individual members know themselves as inherent to the communitarian whole and consciously operate in its ethicised structures, aware that they belong to a universal family established on ethical roots. In this way, we have the supreme recomposition of an organic and living ethicality following the transition through the negative of the system of needs: the latter, which from Adam Smith to today's triumph of liberism, is regarded as the sole and supreme form of society ruled by the competitivism of the atomistic system, is for Hegel the moment of the negative and of the scission that must be overcome.

Thus, once again, it is clear why the ideological logic of absolute capitalism aims at the neutralisation of both the State and of the family, namely, to wipe out any trace of the *sittlich* aspect, of the solidary communitarian dimension: and, in convergent fashion, to elevate the system of needs of individually competitive atoms to an exclusive form of social living, creating post-bourgeois and post-proletarian plebeian multitudes, comprised of solitary individuals with postmodernised consciousnesses and dissolved social ties. The ethical community, both in its original and immediate variant (the family), and in its posited and mediated variant (the State), is dissolved in favour of the non-communitarian community of exchange and of the unsociable sociability of the *do ut des* described by Smith in *Wealth of Nations*.

There is a complete inversion with respect to Hobbes, and a complete return to Aristotle's communitarian ethics: there is no original *status naturae* of agonal competitivism (Hobbes), only the immediate ethical community comprised by the family (Aristotle).

The *state of nature* of Hobbesian memory is secondary and stems from the dispersion of the original community as occurs with the transition to the de-ethicised system of needs: as for Hobbes, also for Hegel *exeundum est e statu naturae* (*we must leave the state of nature*), and this is possible only by reclaiming the ethical, that is, through the re-ethicisation of civil society made possible by the intervention of those ethical powers capable of rekindling the sense of solidary community against anomic and competitive individualism. The egoistic and acquisitive man, rapacious and anti-communitarian, is not the outcome of human nature, as Hobbes unduly portrays him: on the other hand, for Hegel, he is the outcome of the socio-economic process of de-ethicisation of the system of needs ('I think of man in his concept, not in the state-of-nature').[15]

With the Hegelian syntax of the *Science of Logic*, we could say that, in the horizon of ethicality, the family is the concept, civil society is the objectification and, finally, the State is the idea. As already highlighted, civil society as the

15 Hegel, *The Jena Lectures on the Philosophy of Spirit* (Detroit: Wayne State University Press, 1983).

system of needs corresponds to the place of individualistic and competitive fragmentation of the original unity represented by the family community. The unity given and centred on feelings (the family) is divided into the plurality of the dispersed and competitive 'I's: thus, the result is the triumph of the realm of the abstract intellect, which separates what was originally united in immediate form, therefore allowing, in preparatory form, a recomposition to a higher level, because posited and with awareness.

As described in *Elements of the Philosophy of Right*, civil society represents the realm of abstract intellect and of scissions:[16] there is no longer a solidary family-centred community, but only the atomistic system of the competitive monads that have no windows other than those opened by the competitive and utilitarian logic. The two highest manifestations of this logic, established on the prevalence of the abstract intellect are, for Hegel, English political economy (physiologically incapable of understanding the constituting totality), and the subjective moralising peevishness of the titanic abstract intellect, which heightens itself above its own historical horizon without slightly corresponding to its concrete needs (what Hegel, in 1800, ironically described as 'the beatitude in which the I has it all, and all as opposite, under its feet').[17]

In particular, paragraph 183 of *Elements of the Philosophy of Right* outlines the *bürgerliche Gesellschaft* in its lowest

16 Paul Chamley, *Économie Politique et Philosophie chez Steuart et Hegel* (Paris: Dalloz, 1963).

17 *JS*, p. 351.

possible representation – the system of needs – primarily as the 'external state, state of necessity and of intellect' (*äusseren Staat, Not- und Verstandes- staat*). This system of omnilateral dependence and of dispersion of ethicality is consequently rooted in the self-reproductive need of the singularity conceived as an independent atom: at this level, the singular and the universal, the I and society, are connected, but according to modalities that allow them to subsist as independent and disconnected.

The transition from the family to the system of needs as the first figure of civil society thus comprises a temporary abandonment of communitarian ethicality in favour of the individualistic scission: 'this reflective relation therefore initially presents the loss of ethicality'.[18] Ethicality is dissolved in the system of exchange established by the privatistic logic of individuals in search of their own gain, such as the brewer and the butcher discussed by Smith, since civil society, and in particular the system of needs, appears as the 'external state – the state of necessity and of intellect'[19] that disjoins and fragments all.

Dialectical reason, which operates in the State as the fulfillment of the ethical idea in its in-itselfness and for-itselfness, painfully recomposes, by ethicising society, the original innocent union given in family love and in the natural community: the State is thus called upon to overcome the realm of the fractured, dispersed and

18 *GPR*, § 181.

19 Ibid, § 183.

agonistic particularities of civil society as a *system of atomistics*, so that the fabric of society may again be solidary and communitarian, taking the form of a universal family capable of overturning the privatistic logic of the unsociable sociability of the de-ethicised market. In accordance with the definition of the *Encyclopedia* (§ 535), the State is 'self-conscious ethical substance', ethicality that has reached the rank of in-itselfness and for-itselfness: again, in the words of the *Encyclopedia* (§ 517), '*formal universality*' (*formelle Allgemeinheit*) transitions into the real ethical universality, into '*organic reality*' (*organische Wirklichket*).

That the system of needs is pervaded by dissolution and fragmentation is undeniably demonstrated by the rampant social inequality and polarisation which are inherent to it: disproportionate riches accumulate in the hands of a few, the pauperised masses take the form of a deformed populace, and individual acquisitive interest destructures every sense of belonging to the communitarian whole. These considerations offer a glimpse of Hegel's severe critique of capitalism as a triumph of the de-ethicised system of needs, where production prevails as an end-in-itself, parcelled out and abstract, alongside the pauperisation of society and the prevailing of anomic egoism, the genesis of a materially and spiritually poor plebeian class and the triumph of a very restricted caste of property-owners who lack communitarian spirit. In Lukácsian terms, we could say that the 'problems of capitalistic society' do not cease to be acknowledged and denounced as such even by the *mature* Hegel.

If the *young* Hegel at the centre of Lukács' work mostly insisted on the individualistic logic arising from the alienating prose of modern capitalism as a triumph of the de-ethicised system of needs, the *mature* Hegel, without renouncing his earlier acquisitions, focuses more on the hiatus between the atomistic system and the ethical communitarian State. After all, from 1802 onwards, Hegel elaborated the *sittliche Organisation*, or *ethical organisation*,[20] regarding society in an organicistic and non-atomistic way.

In the landscape of the de-ethicised system of needs, there no longer is any trace of the sense of universal unity: only the atom persists with its belief of being itself the universal, conceiving as enemies all that surround it. As previously mentioned, civil society, for Hegel, consequently posits itself as the equivalent of nature: it is, by its very essence, a condition of loss to external accidentality, 'decadence of the idea from itself', where 'the game of forms is victim to a disorderly and unrestrained accidentality', and 'all the accidentality of its existences' undisputedly prevails. It comprises the apotheosis of the 'irrationality of exteriority'.[21]

We must not forget that Hegel criticises the de-ethicised society especially with reference to abhorred England. The latter represents, in every respect, the apogee of the competitive atomistic system, oblivious to any form of

20 Hegel, *Über die wissenschaftlichen Behandlungsarten des Naturrechts*, p. 406.

21 *EPW*, The Philosophy of Nature.

communitarian ethicality. This is what Hegel tells us in his crepuscular article *Über die englische Reformbill*, a ruthless critique of the English constitutional system and, with it, of the 'bestiality of the English pauperised rabble'.[22]

Hegel's critique of England is directed at acquisitive and de-ethicised individualism as the foundation of a non-communitarian and unsociably sociable social being. On English soil, only the formal rights of the acquisitive atom prevail, what Hegel scornfully defines a 'heap of manure of private rights'.[23]

As a consequence, the English constitution, which continuously celebrates and prides itself on the 'pomposity of formal freedom',[24] is by no means the most free of all: indeed, it establishes itself on a merely formal freedom, which coexists with forms of material slavery resulting from the existence of an immense pauperised populace deprived of any rights that are not formal ones, and capable of surviving only as empty forms in the absence of those material rights that England is unable to guarantee.

Therefore, what is at the centre of the English constitution is the de-ethicised freedom of the system of needs, the freedom for landowners to push farmers out of their land by the dozen and to enjoy their profits undisturbed. In other words, it comprises the constitutionalisation of the competitive freedom of the market heightened to only and supreme form of freedom, in the neutralisation of

22 *JS*, p. 307.

23 Ibid, p. 301.

24 Ibid, p. 302.

the *sittlich* element and in the idiosyncrasy for every form of ethical universalism that transcends the boundaries of the individual, ideologically magnified to autocratic atom: 'the individual wishes to depend only on himself in every respect, and refers himself to the universal only through this idiosyncrasy'.[25]

For the English, being free means, in fact, being able to realise without impediments and restrictions their own empirical particularity, in complete oblivion of the dimension of organic solidary community:

> The English are truly proud of the glory and freedom of their nation; the basis of their national pride, however, is the consciousness that in England the individual can preserve and fulfil his particularity.[26]

In this resides, for Hegel, 'the so-called practical sense of the British nation, namely its preoccupation with profit, income and wealth',[27] and nothing else. For this reason, England represents in all respects the triumph of the fractionating abstract intellect in every sphere: theoretically, because it is a people devoid of metaphysics and exclusively dedicated to the forms of intellectualistic knowledge centred on experience; socio-politically, because the English do not recognise the communitarian dimension of *ethical*

25 Hegel, *Philosophy of Mind*, trans. by W. Wallace and A.V. Miller (Oxford: Clarendon Press, 2007), p. 47.

26 Ibid, p. 48.

27 *JS*, p. 307.

totality, absorbed as they are in the particularism of the de-ethicised system of atomistics and in the search for the exclusive realisation of their particularism. In this light, Hegel's sustained hostility towards the English is understandable, with Cromwell being one of the very few figures in English history praised by the Stuttgart philosopher.

The magnified and constitutionalised freedom of the English people is thus the lowest form of freedom, the formal freedom of the competitive individuals of the de-ethicised system of needs. In other terms, by showing – such is the intuition in *Capital* – humanity 'the image of its own future',[28] in the structures of market economy, England is already displaying the structure of absolute post-bourgeois and post-proletarian capitalism that only today can exist in its fully realised form. The solidary ethical community, still partially present in the previous bourgeois and proletarian phase, is dissolved in the new figure of the de-ethicised system of needs populated exclusively by competitive atoms in the form of the self-employed, of the businessman, of the *startupper*. What prevails is *atheism in the ethical world* and freedom conceived as mere pursuit of individual egoistic interests without interference by the State and ethics.

The globalised system of needs in the context of absolute chrematistics, precisely because it is freed from the dimension of ethicality, is more precisely a system of desires: unlike the need, which is congenitally

28 *MEW*, XXIII, p. 14.

finite and limited, the desire has no limits and its essence lies in its inexhaustibility.

If needs can be satisfied, desires, on the other hand, are insatiable and without measure: for this reason, the de-ethicised system of needs is overturned into a system of unlimited and unlimitable desires, which fuels consumerist civilisation as fury of increase and as bad infinite in progress.

Hegel, a bourgeois anticapitalist, mounts his opposition from the point of view of the acquisitions made by the modern world of the bourgeoisie, while Marx – a bourgeois who adheres to the proletarian cause recognising it as the vector of human emancipation from the capitalistic contradiction – will oppose the system from the perspective of the proletariat. Thus in *Encyclopedia* (§ 539):

> Nothing has become more ordinary than the idea that each must limit his freedom in relation to the freedom of others; and that the State is the condition in which this mutual limitation takes place, and the laws are the limits. In these points of view, freedom is conceived only as contingent caprice and arbitrariness.

The English *exemplum* as a realm of the '*out-of-itself*' of the system of needs heightened to the supreme form of social life, allows us to better understand, in a Hegelian way, the process of de-ethicisation consistent with the leaving of the family community and with the not yet accomplished re-ethicisation operated by the State.

The ethical community of individuals with solidarity for the particular universalism of the family has overturned into the universal egoism of the unsociable sociability of uprooted and competitive atoms of the system of needs, according to what can be defined as the 'individualistic atomisation of society':[29] the plebeian realm produced by the centrifugal forces of the acquisitive individualism that disjoins the solidary community. Thus Hegel writes in *Encyclopedia* (§ 523):

> The substance, which, as spirit, abstractly particularises itself into many people [...] loses its ethical character; for these people do not have in their consciousness and for their purpose absolute unity, but their own particularity and their being-for-themselves: whence the atomistic system is born. The substance becomes for this reason nothing more than a universal connection and mediator of independent extremes and of their particular interests.

In its figure of system of needs, civil society, not yet permeated by the ethical roots of the State and no longer held firm by the immediate ethicality of the family community, stands as the republic of private and competitive interests, and therefore as the space of a competition that binds individuals according to the logic of individual triumph over others and not of community solidarity.

29 Preve, *La Quarta Guerra Mondiale* (Parma: Insegna del Veltro, 2008), p. 91.

Civil society becomes a mere projection on the surface of competitive, de-politicised, de-ethicised economy: a return to the *status naturae* and to its *bellum omnium contra omnes*, declaring at the outset as noxious any attempt to leave it. The community dissolves into individual atomistics and polarises into the two extremes of the caste of the rich and the caste of the wretched plebeians, what Hegel repeatedly and vibrantly denounces. This is what comprises the model of hegemonic society in England, to which Adam Smith has conferred philosophical-political dignity:

> It is certainly not from the benevolence of the butcher, the brewer or the baker that we expect our lunch, but from the fact that they take care of their interest. We do not turn to their humanity but to their egoism and we never speak to them of our needs, but of their gains. No one who is not a beggar ever chooses to depend above all on the benevolence of his fellow citizens, and even a beggar does not depend exclusively on it.[30]

Such a model of society built on non-social and, moreover, on programmatically unsociable foundations, is based on the acquisitive drive of egoisms and, according to Smith's theorem, on the inscrutable action of a sensibly supersensible entity – the unexplained that explains all, the *invisible hand* – which, by immanentising the device

30 Adam Smith, *The Wealth of Nations* (London: Penguin, 2003).

of transcendence, operates as a worldly God, guaranteeing the emergence of public virtues from private vices, and the victory of the common good over the merely egoistic one.

This is how Marx, in *Capital*, summarises with a veiled but scathing irony, the Smithsonian sophism of the invisible hand as the engine of the presumptive social good, with respect to which the Trier thinker, following in Hegel's footsteps, reveals himself to be soberly agnostic:

> Each looks only to himself. The only force that brings them together and puts them in relation is that of *their own profit, their particular advantage, and their private interests* (*ihres Eigennutzes, ihres Sondervorteils, ihrer Privatinteressen*). And precisely because each one looks to himself only, and no one bothers about the rest, do they all, in agreement with a pre-established harmony of things, or under the auspices of an all-shrewd providence, work together to their mutual advantage, for common profit, and the interest of all.[31]

There is no solidarity, nor sense of belonging, not even communitarian spirit: society, at this level, is given only as the resulting atomistics of a system of omnilateral dependency arising from Robinsonian individual need and competitivism, and aided by the imponderable doing of an immanent providence, from which we can deduce, again with Marx, the unspoken similarity between market

31 *MEW*, XXIII, p. 190.

economy and religion, between political economy and theology.

Hegel demystifies Smith's theorem, outlining how the de-ethicised system of needs, far from producing the general good, favours the dissolution of the communitarian fabric and the increasing pauperisation of parts of the population, which lose their fundamental rights, including that of existence.

Theorised by Smith in its most complete form, the new paradigm of the non-sociable society, homogeneous to the world of production and of circulation of commodities, is preceded by Hobbes' theoretical system. The very frontispiece of *Leviathan* (1651) efficaciously outlines the new, bluntly anti-Aristotelian, perspective of society as resulting from the aggregation of autonomous and prioritarian individuals, who by convention choose the *exitus* from the *status naturae* and work together to better protect, in social form, their own individual interests, above all the personal *securitas*.

For Hobbes, prior to the *pactum unionis*, there is no element of communitarian solidarity: there is only a disjoined and inconsistent *multitudo*, inhabited by individuals who are infinitely desiring and intrinsically competitive and antagonistic, ready to go to war against each other in view of the protection of their own personal interest. The condition is not that of the Aristotelian solidary community, but that of the 'cloudy sky' that menaces rain and storm. The individual as a social atom chooses, therefore, to abandon his solitude to better protect his own anti-communitarian individuality, adhering to the *pactum unionis* in the form of a *pactum subiectionis* tended to universally neutralise the conflicting pressures that threaten its existence in the state of nature.

The modern subject, inhabitant of the system of needs in search of its own complete de-ethicisation, is founded on the complete overturning of the Aristotelian anthropology of man as a political, sociable and communitarian animal (ζῷον πολιτικὸν).

Initially, with Descartes, the subject is conceived as an abstractly calculating and concretely de-socialised atom. Later, with Hobbes, it appears as a conflictual and anti-communitarian monad. Then, with Locke's *Second Treatise of Civil Government* (1690), it already acquires the Robinsonian form of *homo oeconomicus*, of ideal inhabitant of the system of needs which, although not yet fully de-ethicised, has already largely subordinated the political sphere to the economic one. Society and the State, if still permitted, have become simple containers of completion, recognition and protection of the de-ethicised system of needs, now heightened to only possible source of social life. The Aristotelian perspective has been turned upside down.

If Thomas Aquinas, in his *Summa Theologiae*, could still uphold a theological-political perspective of priority by the communitarian totality over the parts (*totalitas ante partes*) and assert, in Aristotle's footsteps, that *the law is an ordering of reason aimed at the common good, and promulgated by he who has the care of the community* (*lex est quaedam rationis ordinatio ad bonum commune, ab eo qui curam communitatis habet promulgate*, I-II, q. 90, a. 4), in Robinsonian modernity law and politics increasingly tend to be redefined according to the economy and, more precisely, to the system of needs.

For the modern anti-communitarian subject, victim of the *atheism in the ethical world* and diligent curator of his own individual interest, in the utmost irresponsible lack of responsibility towards the rest of the world (so as to prefer, with Hume's example, 'the destruction of the whole world to the scratching of my finger'),[32] words such as those at the centre of Aristotle's *Politics*, on the communitarian spirit of the *polis*, could seem without a foundation and, perhaps, to not even make sense any more:

> The community of the city is not only defined by the locality, by the abstinence from mutual harm and by the safeguarding of commercial relations, because, although these things are essential for the existence of the city, even if they are all realised, this is not yet a city, as the city is the community that guarantees good life to families and clans, and its purpose is an independent and perfect life.[33]

The perspective of Aristotle's *Politics* – which, essentially, confers dignity and thought to the entire Greek ethics

32 David Hume, *A Treatise of Human Nature* (New York: Fordham University Press, 1995).

33 Aristotle, *Politics* (Newburyport: Focus Pub., 2012).

and to the spirit of communitarianism that characterised it – precedes Hegel's ethical system, also centred on the communitarian element, or κοινονία, intended in such a way so as to allow prevalence of τὸ κοινὸν, *the common*.

Even Hegel, in *Elements of the Philosophy of Right*, as Aristotle in *Politics*, begins from the family as a natural community immediately given: it constitutes the proof that man is born in the community and only in this can he develop as a man, in antithesis to the Robinsonian and contractualist perspectives of modern men, who seek in various ways, through *necessary false consciousness*, to absolutise the moment of the system of needs, naturalising it (*id est* heightening it in Hobbesian and Lockean way to the super-temporal level of *status naturae*) and conceiving the State and politics as mere guarantors of its primacy (according to the English model and its constitutionalisation of the freedom of the system of needs promoted as the only one possible).

Hegel's communitarian perspective, with its revived Greek cultural heritage, is metaphysically grounded in the very conception of Spirit found at the centre of the *Phenomenology*: the *Geist* is characterised as intrinsically communitarian, since it is 'the I that is We, and the We that is I';[34] and, therefore, absolute circularity between the singularised individual I and the social collective I as the resultant dynamics of the empirical 'I's that know

34 Hegel, 'Phänomenologie des Geistes, 1807', *Schriften und Entwürfe (1799-1808)*, IX (Leipzig: Meiner, 1998), p. 108.

themselves to be constituent parts of the intersubjective community.

Again, with the syntax of the *Phenomenology of Spirit*, *Geist* is 'absolute substance which, in the perfect freedom and autonomy of its own opposition, that is, of the different self-consciousnesses existent for-themselves, constitutes the unity of the very self-consciousness'.[35] Using a varied mix of ontology and political philosophy, Hegel rejects the individualism rampant throughout the course of Robinsonian modernity and upholds a communitarian vision of the Spirit: a vision by virtue of which the object, the thing, 'is a thing only as the activity of each and everyone, it is the essence that constitutes the essence of all essences'.[36] Moreover, the thing, 'through the work of each and everyone, is produced as their unity and equality':[37] in this resides 'the meaning that the thing acquires as social being'.[38]

In this perspective, centred on the 'sociality of reason as a community of free beings',[39] for which, as highlighted by Masullo, 'Hegel ultimately wants to express that the foundation of the world lies in inter-subjectivity',[40] the existent is always conceived in social terms as a reality of each

35 Ibid.

36 Ibid, p. 227.

37 Ibid.

38 Ibid.

39 Luigi Ruggiu, *Lo Spirito è Tempo. Saggi su Hegel* (Milan: Mimesis 2013), p. 275.

40 Aldo Masullo, 'Il Fondadamento Comunitario', in *La Potenza della Scissione* (Naples: Edizioni scientifiche italiane, 1997), p. 62.

and everyone, as individual and collective consciousness or, more precisely, as a communitarian dimension:

> The thing is itself the universal that constitutes a being only insofar as it is activity of each and everyone, and it is a reality because it knows this consciousness as its own reality and as the reality of all.[41]

By knowingly overcoming Descartes' transcendental solipsism, as well as Hobbes' individualistic egoism, and Locke's acquisitive one, Hegel insists on the fact that, in the social sphere, there can be freedom only where there is a community of free entities, and that, metaphysically, self-consciousness is given only in the mutual recognition of self-consciousnesses: 'self-consciousness is in-itself and for-itself only insofar as it is in-itself and for-itself for another self-consciousness, that is, only insofar as it is something that is recognised'.[42]

Proof of the markedly ideological character, in the Marxian sense, of the contractualistic position and of its tacit aspiration to present the competitive atomistic system as naturally given and, therefore, to be prioritised over any other social relation (including the one existing within the framework of the State), is found, in Hegel's opinion, in the very idea of a *social contract*: the figure of the contract is typical of private law and, therefore, of the sphere of civil society.

41 Hegel, 'Phänomenologie des Geistes, 1807', p. 228.
42 Ibid, p. 137.

It is an act of intellectual barbarism wishing to apply this figure to the dimension of public law, pretending that the genesis of the State should be identified in a contract: it is on these grounds, in the *Philosophy of Right* (§ 258), that Hegel unconditionally rejects the perspective according to which 'the association of individuals in the State becomes a contract'. Moreover, from 1802, that is, from his written work *Über die wissenschaftlichen Behandlungsarten des Naturrechts*, Hegel firmly denounces that, with Hobbes and the heterogeneous school of contractualists, 'the form of such a subordinate private relation' has barbarically entered 'the absolute majesty of ethical totality',[43] by its nature irreducible to any form of private contractualisation.

This is what Hegel, in *Lectures on the History of Philosophy*, never misses the opportunity to reiterate, also against Rousseau, who, even if moving from a genuine tension towards a solidary community, ends up, *volens nolens*, assuming the same unjustified contractualist presupposition, and subsequently, the illuministic one that regards society and the State as deriving from the *a posteriori* union of individual atoms already complete in themselves: 'the State is not a union that is bound by the will of individuals'.

In antithesis to the English nation and to its surreptitious heightening of the de-ethicised system of needs to *non plus ultra* of social living, Hegel prioritises the re-ethicisation of civil society, so that it may be saved from the competitive

43 Hegel, *Über die wissenschaftlichen Behandlungsarten des Naturrechts*, p. 405.

scission to return to its ethical roots which, central to the family community, have been lost with the dependence on the system of needs.

For this reason, the subsequent figures of civil society, in *Elements of the Philosophy of Right*, are tasked with beginning the process for reclaiming the community *ethos* and the spirit of belonging to the ethical universe. In the system of de-ethicised needs, as in England, dominates the figure of the *Atheismus der sittlichen Welt*, '*atheism of the ethical world*',[44] that is, the loss of interest for the question of communitarian truth and the consequent exclusive attachment to the particularity of the competitive I.

If the system of needs is the first, and lowest, figure of ethicality, the two subsequent ones already signal the emergence of ethical roots and the return of the *sittlich* element: these figures correspond to *a*) the administration of justice, *b*) the police and the corporation. In particular, the *police*, intended in the eighteenth-century sense as *administration*, considerably strengthens the link between the I and the communitarian whole, repressing lesion of right and preventing its violations. Already operational, during this phase, are the ethical roots, which control the economic and agonal competitivism, guaranteeing education and material rights and preventing the formation of a plebeian caste and the pauperisation of the masses.

In the system of ethicality, the police not only performs tasks related to public order, it also safeguards concrete

44 *GPR*, p. 14.

measures of economic politics set out by the government: for example, it reduces the prices of primary goods, it intervenes where a single company is put into risk by the market and, more generally, it protects the internal economic provision. The latter has as its objective the reduction of the duration of the *convulsions* (*Zuckungen*) of the internal market. In this sense, with Hegel's syntax, *police* explicitly refers not to the modern repressive institution aimed at the maintaining of order, but to social policy, intended as art of the *polis*, looking after the welfare of citizens, bearers of rights and of duties.

When the police cannot intervene, the corporation does. The latter displays an even greater, operative presence of a cohesive organic whole, albeit limited to the category of those who undertake a specific type of work. As the anticipation, in many respects, of what would then become the trade union and mutualistic associations, the corporation stands as a community of life that guarantees solidarity in the face of possible misery: with the police and, to a greater extent, with the corporation, 'the ethical sphere returns to civil society as an immanent'.[45]

The scission of the de-ethicised system of needs is overcome through the recomposition of the solidary ethical community. The State stands, for Hegel, as the fulfillment of ethicality, as the power that actively guarantees the primacy of the organic community, in the spaces of which, every citizen, as a member of the universal family, holds imprescriptible material and formal rights.

45 Ibid, § 249.

In antithesis to the *vulgata* and the raving visions which portray Hegel not only as an apologist of the historical process, exclusively identified with rationality – when in fact it is Hegel himself, in *Encyclopedia* (§ 6 A.), to remind us that not all that is, deserves the 'emphatic name of real' simply because it is – but also as intrinsically *totalitarian* (according to the Popperian inquisitorial paradigm of the hunt for the *enemies of open society*), the Stuttgart thinker conceives the State not as a totality negating the value of individuals, but as an ethical organism that allows full expressivity and complete realisation within the framework of the solidary community.

If the freedom of the ancient community, although great, was only objective and found its theorisation in Plato, and if the moderns only knew subjective freedom, from Christianity to Luther, up to the Kantian accomplishment, Hegel believes to have found a virtuous synthesis: the ethical State is orderly equilibrium of objective freedom and subjective freedom, since, as the perfect realisation of ethicality, it posits itself as objective ethical totality, as *ethical universe* (*sittliches Universum*) in which individuals recognise themselves subjectively.[46]

After digesting some theoretical plexuses of Rousseau's

46 Against competitive privatism, 'Hegel formulates an administration destined to decide independently of the pressure on society, on the basis of rational criteria inspired by the common good, because, unlike in antiquity, the Hegelian State retains subjective freedom, it must grant it, if anything, the place that it deserves'. Henning Ottman, *Individuum und Gemeinschaft bei Hegel*, I, *Hegel im Spiegel der Interpretationen* (Berlin: De Gruyter, 1977), p. 291.

political reflection, Hegel is thinking, with the category of ethical State, of an ethicised people, which obeys the law by obeying itself: according to what has been explicated ever since his earlier writings, 'the absolute ethical totality is no other than a people'.[47] Obedient will is free, since it obeys itself, it freely submits to the ethical power of the State, to the *sittliches Universum* in which it fully realises itself. In this sense, the State, with the categories of the *Philosophy of Right* (§ 260), is 'the reality of concrete freedom', the ethicality in-itself and for-itself reclaimed following the scission put into being by the system of needs.

Therefore, the intervention of the ethicising State is necessary for the re-establishment of the communitarian and solidary ethics: the individual particularity is left free, since civil society is not abolished with the State. Instead, what is suppressed is the need by the individual to be valued and recognised as an isolated atom, without ties to the social totality of which it is part:

> Here the interest of the idea [...] is the process of raising the singularity [...] to formal freedom and to the formal universality of knowledge and will, of forming subjectivity in their [of needs] particularity.[48]

The singularity is not abolished, but 'raised' to universal and substantial freedom, without any weakening of the

47 Hegel, *Über die wissenschaftlichen Behandlungsarten des Naturrechts*, p. 371.

48 *GPR*, § 187

element of particularity, which is, instead, strengthened by the presence of ethical roots.

Thus Hegel, although he harshly criticises the *modus operandi* of natural law, agrees with its fundamental orientation, that is, the justification of the rationality of the State (*extra rem publicam nulla salus, outside the State there is no salvation*), following a theme that coherently accompanies his political reflection. As we know, Hegel composed and restructured the system of right and of the State for approximately thirty years, producing at least eight editions: four in Jena, one in Nuremberg, the three public ones of Heidelberg, and two in Berlin. There are various and not secondary remodellings, although Hegel's political philosophy – 'conservative in style, progressive in content'[49] – never questions the centrality of the State as ethical power and as realisation of communitarian life.

Through the ethicisation of society implemented by the State, Hegel thinks a political community that is the *telos* of agency by equally free and solidary citizens: there is no subordination of the individual, but, on the contrary, full right by each citizen to participate in the political decisions of the State. The Hegelian conception at the centre of the *Philosophy of Right* (§ 258), according to which 'the individual himself has objectivity, truth and ethicality only insofar as he is a component of the State', must be understood in this hermeneutical key: the individual fully realises himself in his free individuality only in the ethical

49 H. Lübbe, 'Hegel critico della società politicizzata' in *Il pensiero politico di Hegel*, ed. by Claudio Cesa (Rome: Laterza, 1979), p. 157.

community and, therefore, only in the State as living ethical idea.

The freedom of the individual remains, for Hegel, an indispensable value, the implementation of which can only be given within the framework of an ethical community of solidary individuals who are equally free. For this reason, Hegel assimilates and remodels, in his own system, and in original form, the freedom of the private individual (according to the legacy left by the Enlightenment), the inner freedom of consciousness (fruit of the Christian tradition) and, finally, the social freedom guaranteed by ethical powers, which allow the full development of the individual as a member of the organic community. This should in itself be enough to refute Mario Rossi's thesis, according to which the part in Hegel's system related to politics and the State would appear as the 'most reactionary part, at least in its conclusions, of Hegelian philosophy'.[50]

On the contrary, against the *locus communis* according to which there is, in Hegel, an unjustified deification of the State, it may be asserted that his system proposes a fruitful undeification of the economy and of the de-ethicised system of needs: an undeification that, directed mainly against the England of his time, allows today to direct a critique at the hegemonic logic of planetary *laissez-faire* as the ideology of the de-ethicised system of needs, deprived both of the figure of the family and of the figure of the State.

50 Mario Rossi, *Marx e la Dialettica Hegeliana. I, Hegel e lo Stato* (Rome: Editori Riuniti, 1960), p. 30.

Thanks to its prevalence, there is today a new rising figure of civil society, which is increasingly freed from the regulated space of the national State and increasingly defined in global, trans-national and *transactional* terms, centred on the absolutised value of free entrepreneurship without borders and of the competitiveness of the free market, thus no longer limited by political norms and by principles of ethicality, which are now dissolved in the system of globalised competitive atomistics.

Therefore, Topitsch's formula, according to which 'every political praxis may be justified with Hegelian arguments' does not seem convincing:[51] 'political praxis', today hegemonic, aimed at depriving of a foundation every residual communitarian entity so that the logic of the de-ethicised system of needs and of the unregulated market may ubiquitously prevail, not only may not be justified with Hegelian arguments, but may actively be attacked with them.

In general, the most distinctive aspect of the *Sittlichkeit* is its affective and sentimental stability, which is condensed in the institution of marriage and family life. It is also characterised by a working stability, identified in the permanent place of work guaranteed by a contract. Furthermore, another characteristic aspect is its existential stability, guaranteed to individuals as citizens members of the universal family, corresponding to civil society.

51 Ernst Topitsch, 'Kritik der Hegel-Apologeten' in Gerd-Klaus Kaltenbrunner, *Hegel und die Folgen* (Freiburg: Rombach, 1970), pp. 329-360.

The communitarian ethicality thematised by Hegel concerns individuals inserted within communitarian ties and connected to the *ethos* of a historically determined people. These ties, however, do not correspond to those of the *ancien régime* feudal society, being instead modern, as they presuppose freedom of consciousness attained by the individual.

For this reason, the community conceived by Hegel is posited as an overcoming of both the feudal totality in the absence of recognition for individualities, and of the competitive atomistic fragmentation produced by the Enlightenment. It is structured in the form of a community which is respectful of individuals, who are realised in the living relation that puts them in dynamic connection with the communitarian fabric to which they concretely belong.

As Hegel clarifies with reference to the existence of individuals in ethical life, 'the institutions themselves guarantee them, in the corporation, an occupation and activity directed towards a universal purpose',[52] allowing 'the foresight and determination of work for all through public organisation'.[53] As discussed in *Elements of the Philosophy of Right*, ethicality is 'the idea of freedom in the sense of *the living good (das lebendige Gute)*',[54]

52 *GPR*, § 264.
53 Ibid, § 236.
54 Ibid, § 142.

the 'concept of freedom turned into given world and nature of self-consciousness'.[55]

As previously pointed out, it is no longer the moment of pure formal abstraction of abstract right and of its coercive exteriority, nor is it the moment of morality as an inner and conscious subjectivity in antithesis to the logics of the given world. On the contrary, ethicality, by overcoming the two preceding moments in a higher synthesis, consists in a concrete and communitarian freedom, in the *ethos* of a people that lives without the scission between interiority and exteriority, in the laws and customs with which it organises its own public life, recognising itself in both single individualities and in the community as a living spirit.

After all, *ethics*, even in our language, etymologically refers to *ethos*, to customs, in the same way that in Hegel's language *Sittlichkeit* refers to *Sitten*, the concrete historical *customs*. Customs may only exist in the context of a community and of an intersubjective relation, where an abstract individual, perhaps imagined as a sort of Philoctetes abandoned on a rock in the middle of the sea, may not have an ethics, devoid as he is of customs.

Then, ethics alludes to that set of institutions (the family, civil society, the State) in which freedom is socially attained by objectifying itself, that is, it gradually transitions from its individualistic abstract expression to the historically concrete universality of the actual existence of a truly

55 Ibid.

existing community, situated in time and space, rooted in the past and projectually open to the future. With Hegel, freedom ceases to be a moral postulate of the idle soul and becomes given reality in the historical-social world, in the concrete realisations of a people operating within the framework of the ethicised and ethicising State.

In Hegel's words, 'ethical powers govern the life of individuals and have their representation, their figure and phenomenical reality, precisely in individuals as their contingencies' (§ 145).[56] The Robinsonian abstract individualism typical of the Enlightenment is dialectically overturned into a concrete, communitarian and historically determined ethics. In such an ethics, the individual is projected into the concreteness of intersubjective and communitarian relations that make him, with Aristotle's *Politics* (I A, 2, 1253a3), a ζῷον πολιτικòν, a political, sociable and communitarian animal.

56 Ibid, § 145.

6

THE FAMILY AS THE ORIGINAL ETHICAL COMMUNITY

> 'Initially it is the family that constitutes the substantial Whole whose task it is to provide for this particular aspect of the individual'.
>
> (Georg W. F. Hegel, *Elements of the Philosophy of Right*)

As already stated in Aristotle's *Politics* (I, 2, 1252b 14), the family is the first community: 'the community that is constituted for daily life according to nature is the family' (I, 2, 1252 b 14). It is the proof – against the modern Robinsonades, from Thomas Hobbes to Margaret Thatcher – that man is a communitarian animal, that only in the community can he exist and that he is born within it.

In the words of Aristotle, starting from the family, it becomes clear that the community is πρότερον τῇ φύσει, 'comes first by nature' with respect to the individual, who is therefore, by his very essence, a sociable, political and communitarian animal: 'it is therefore evident that the community exists by nature and that it comes before each individual' (*Politics*, I, 2, 1253 to 25).

Aristotle's perspective, which condenses the essence of Greek ethics and of the spirit of communitarianism (and which, as we have said, will be revived, albeit in a different way, by Hegel) stands as the antithesis *ante litteram* of the modern and illuministic vision of society as an atomistic aggregate of competitive and unsociably sociable individualities.

The fact that Aristotle's *Politics* and, *mutatis mutandis*, Hegel's *Elements of the Philosophy of Right* both begin from the family as the foundation of communitarian life is anything but accidental: man is born out of the community and is, consequently, by his essence, a communitarian animal. On its part, the community is not generated by individuals, but it is what generates them; who exist, in their free individuality, as children of the community, above all of the family community.

Following Aristotle, and in antithesis to the Hobbesian narrative, the community does not arise from the union of autonomous individuals already formed and stipulating a *pactum unionis*: it is only the original intersubjective space that allows the genesis and the development of individuals. The logic of the development of modern capitalism, ever since its inception, corresponds to the annihilation of the community and of its solidary ethics and to the redefinition of society in unsociably sociable forms centred on the anthropological figure of the individual without ties other than those dictated by the *auri sacra fames* and from privatistic acquisitive impulse.

For this reason, in its dynamics of de-ethicisation of the world of life, capital today aspires in every way to destroy the family and, with it, every residual form of community, replacing it with isolated and single atoms, unable to speak and understand any other language that is not the Anglophone language of market economy. The de-ethicisation promoted by the flexible post-bourgeois, post-proletarian and super-capitalistic order is therefore based on the annihilation of the communitarian bourgeois and proletarian dimension, in view of the privatistic and competitiveindividualisationofliferedefinedasaneconomic *bellum omnium contra omnes*, as a mere competitive space of free exchange for mutually antagonistic atoms animated by the only rule of the *mors tua, vita mea.*

Modern ethicality, accompanied by capital in the dialectical phase, is today incompatible with the nihilistic and unlimited expansion of the commodity form and of financial economy. For this reason, today's economic fanaticism, in order to impose itself in absolute and free form, must de-ethicise life, annihilating the State and the family, stable work, school and university education. It must make every reality liquid and temporary, flexible and wavering, always re-programmable and re-definable by the needs of production and exchange. It must, indeed, dissolve the sphere that Hegel defined as *Sittlichkeit*, centred on solidary relations between free individualities which are projected into the spaces of the community through the primacy of politics on the economy and of the social dimension on the privatistic one.

In the family, as in love, both studied by the young Hegel in his so-called *theological* writings, and in particular in the *fragment on love*, individual unity ceases to be individual, against the disjoining logics of market-driven modernity. If these logics detach the individual from the community, in love and in family life one experiences a dual truth.

In an actual dual opening, there is thus a sort of fracture of the self so that one may pass through the other. The result is a life lived no longer from the point of view of one, but rather of two, in the form of a molecule of the community that is impermeable to the mercantile relation of the *do ut des*. In this sense, in antithesis to the disjoining logics of acquisitive individualism, of solitary *jouissance* and of rampant affective isolationism, love, driven by the nostalgia of the whole, creates a living totality that is respectful of the irreducible differences between lovers: with Plato, 'being midway between, it makes each to supplement the other, so that the Whole is combined in one' (*Symposium*, 202 e).

Flexible capital does not accept the existence of solidary communities detached from the mercantile relation between competitive and de-ethicised individuals. For this reason, it cannot tolerate the existence of the ethical institution of the family. In the affective relation that binds a mother and a father to the child there is no place for the mercantile logic, from which it remains structurally excluded: free love and disinterested altruism are the only sources of meaning of such relation, structurally antithetical with respect to the algid axiomatic of profit and calculation.

The same love that binds lovers as a genetic cell of the community of the family is incommensurable with any calculation and with any economic figure: it stands as pure givenness that does not neutralise nor reduce the other, but that produces a dual unit which is respectful of differences and vocationally non-egoistic.

For this reason, the love algorithm both intended as *passionate love* (ἔρως) and as *charitable love* (ἀγάπη) can be identified in the formula *volo ut sis* employed by Augustine (*Confessions*, VI, 7, 12) as an emblem of a loving altruism which is also willing to sacrifice one's life for the sake of the beloved. Love is, in this way, pure ontological givenness, a will that makes the loved one be and potentially be. This is what Aristotle writes in his *Nicomachean Ethics* on the emotional bond that unites mother and child:

> Mothers take pleasure from loving their children [...], they carry on loving them even without expecting to be loved in return, and, if both are not possible, it seems that it is enough for them to know that they are well, and they love them even if their children, not knowing their own mother,

> do not return the love that is appropriate
> for a mother.[1]

The unconditional and disinterested love that exists between mothers and their children is also the one that, conversely, the latter reserve for those who have put them into the world, as Cordelia's story paradigmatically tells us in *King Lear*. The unconditional nature of her love emerges from the lack of correspondence, and also, from the real disadvantages that arise from it: 'what shall Cordelia speak? Love, and be silent' (*King Lear*, I, 1, 68).

Love is the recognition that only through the connection with what in appearance is other than the self, can the self constitute itself. In Hegelian way, love is the proof that the individual finds his own truth in the living intersubjective relation and not in his own abstract solitude, proof also of the fact that mankind is capable of disinterested altruism and of unconditional givenness.

Love, in Hegel's early writings, also known as *Early Theological Writings* (where, in truth, the theme of the community is much more central than that of religion, which is itself subordinate to it), is the overcoming of the fracture, the return of the multiplicity to unity, as well as the structural need for unity. Love, says Hegel, is 'feeling of the whole',[2] desire for unity and for totality. The family, conceived in *Elements* as the first moment of ethical life, is the concrete realisation of love, its condensing and

1 Aristotle, *Nicomachean Ethics* (London: University of Chicago Press, 2012), VIII, 1159 a.

2 *JS*, p. 379.

institutionalising at the ethical level. As the concretisation of love, the family is the ethical institution that allows lovers to exist in their irrepressible singularity and, at the same time, as parts of a communitarian totality given by their living relation:

> The objective starting point is people's free consent: and this precisely involves the consent to *constitute a single person* (*eine Person auszumachen*), to renounce, in their unity, their natural and singular personality. In this perspective, marital unity is certainly a self-limitation: however, precisely because both people attain their own substantial self-consciousness, it is their *liberation* (*Befreiung*).[3]

In the couple, the two members realise themselves by self-limitation, establishing a bond that constitutes a single person: this forms the dual truth previously mentioned.[4] They freely limit themselves or, if we prefer, they spontaneously constrain each other to put in place a new ethical bond that makes them into one person, even in the irrepressible singularity that each one does not cease to be. Formerly separated, they now exist as united, in the new solidary and ethical sentiment of the family bond that makes them parts of a living totality. Thus Hegel writes: 'the family predisposition consists in having the self-consciousness of one's individuality in this unity as in

3 *GPR*, § 162.

4 Siebert, *Hegel's Concept of Marriage and Family. The Origin of Subjective Freedom*.

the essentiality existing in-itself and for-itself, so that one exists in it not as a person for-himself, but as a member'.[5]

A micro-community is established, in which the individual does not disappear, but becomes a member of a solidary and non-economic totality in which he can fully realise himself as an individual. The stable, heterosexual, monogamous family presents, certainly, the not rare pathologies of hypocrisy and adultery, as well as of male arrogance; which must be condemned, without this being the pretext for the delegitimisation of the institution of the family itself, corresponding, with Hegel, to the 'highest totality of which nature is capable'.[6]

The family is, according to Hegel, a natural totality, because it may present itself as the communitarianism brought to its minimal cell, to the dual relation.[7] For this reason, as for communitarianism, even for family love the primary enemy is irresponsible egoism, which forgets others and the world in the name of that individual Robinsonian ego which wants to impose its identity against the difference, and its singularised world against the common world.

Hegel writes: 'the unity of marriage, insofar as it is substantial, is only intimacy and predisposition; insofar as it is existing, however, it is distributed among the two

5 *GPR*, § 158.

6 Lasson, p. 445.

7 Eva Bockenheimer, *Hegels Familien- und Gechlechtertheorie* (Hamburg: Meiner, 2013).

subjects'.[8] They feel as one and, at the same time, they are two, united by a giving and non-economic bond that makes them seek the unity of life projects and prospects: to live as if they were *one person*.

The 'natural difference of the sexes',[9] is also given as a difference of 'intellectual and ethical determination',[10] making the masculine and the feminine structurally ἕτεροι, *other*, and, at the same time, such as to give themselves in complementary form: bearers of equal dignity, they complement each other. The ontological difference between man and woman is what guarantees their complementarity and what allows to establish the family community as a founding cell of the social being of man, conceived by Hegel, following in Aristotle's footsteps, as ζῷον πολιτικòν, a political, sociable and communitarian animal. According to Locke's definition, marriage coincides with a voluntary pact between man and woman, consisting 'first of all in that communion and in that mutual right over bodies which serves its primary purpose: procreation'.[11] The *mutual right* evoked by Locke alludes to a relationship of biunivocal recognition, of equal dignity and respect.

The search of unity by the ἕτεροι produces, when it is attained, a *substantial unity* that does not neutralise the otherness of the two sexes, but that accomplishes it in the new living duality of the family relation, in the 'ethical

8 *GPR*, § 173.

9 Ibid, § 161.

10 Ibid.

11 John Locke, *Second Treatise of Government* (New York: John Wiley & Sons, 2014).

relation' of monogamous marriage as an 'undivided bond' founded on 'corporeal union' and, above all, on the 'commonality of personal and particular interests'.[12]

To animate the bond of love is not only the corporeal union or the natural attraction between man and woman, but also the commonality of interests and passions, of the projects and perspectives that ties the couple together and that conducts it, through marriage, to attain a stable and solid relation in the form of a continuously renewed choice. The sentiment and the projectuality that ties them together can thus be stabilised in the ethical form of married life.

With Hegel, the otherness of the male and female sex finds its unification in ethical family life, understood not as the neutralisation of the difference, but as the attainment of unity in the difference or, if we prefer, as a dual synthesis in which the different coexist in unity. However, its highest level and as a synthesis of love, unity is concretely achieved only with the birth of children, who are the unity in which the couple transform their aspirations of full union into reality. In other words, the desire for unity becomes living through the generation of the child, a synthesis of the dual aspect in search of its unitary dimension. Through the child, the couple finds its aspiration to unity, which has become a concrete and living reality:

> In children, this unity becomes *an existence existing for itself* (*eine für sich seiende Existenz*) and an object that the spouses

12 Ibid.

love as their love, as their substantial existence.[13]

In the child, the spouses recognise their love, the fruit of the encounter and of the desired existential unity: the child, as a synthesis of the love of the two spouses exists as *existence existing for itself*, endowed with autonomous life, thus positing as the fulfillment of the unity that the two lovers were searching for and that until then had obtained without being able to transcend the ontological difference that separated them and that made each one an unsurpassable singularity. This love is also determined in what Hegel describes as the 'second birth of the children',[14] coinciding with their *spiritual birth*, that is, with their education as *autonomous people*, as human beings in the full sense, according to a project which, initiated by the family, will then be continued by civil society as a *universal family*, through educational institutions of the scholastic type.

Family love and family life are disinterested and altruistic. In the love relation, but also in the emotional bond that unites mother and child, there is no place for the logic of economic fanaticism and for the *do ut des*: there exists a tie of pure unconditional solidarity, a giving logic that by its very nature already disputes the market economy and the commercialisation of all relations. For this reason, absolute and post-bourgeois capital hates the family and love, understood both as an erotic bond (ἔρως) and as

13 *GPR*, § 173.

14 Ibid, § 170.

pure giving affectivity (ἀγάπη). Economic fundamentalism substitutes the family with atomic individuals unified only by the liturgy of free trade, that is, the *system of atomistics* denounced by Hegel in his *Encyclopedia*.

It replaces familiarly ethicised love with that alienated substitute that is 'liquid love',[15] with those relationships consisting of pure individual self-gratification, in which the other is only a pretext for the self-referential pleasure of the I detached from the communitarian fabric as the fragmented unrelated plurality of isolated atoms.

In the transition from the bourgeois to the post-bourgeois phase of the de-ethicised and flexible system of needs, the stabilised ethical union of the family, established on the ontological difference between man and woman, is replaced by the liberal-libertarian erotic deregulation for undifferentiated atoms that give rise to ephemeral and precarious aggregates, which never settle into lasting forms able to transcend momentary pleasure.

The ideological delegitimisation of the heterosexual family as the foundation of communitarian life centred on the ethicisation of the sentimental relation, and therefore on its stability, occurs through the actions of the postmodern *oratores* as mediators of consensus: who ridicule it and, at the same time, demonise it as intrinsically authoritarian and chauvinist, as vocationally homophobic and oppressive. On the other hand, they recite the eulogy of the unregulated forms of postmodern, ephemeral and flexible eroticism,

15 Zygmunt Bauman, *Liquid Love. On the Frailty of Human Bonds* (Oxford: Blackwell, 2003).

dissolved from any ethicised communitarian dimension, and functional to consumeristic atoms which, through commodity-objects as through commodity-pleasures, individually and solitarily relate to the otherness for the sole purpose of always reconfirming their narcissistic I in search of surplus-*jouissance* without limits or restrictions.

Even in this case, the analogy between the forms of neoliberal sociality and the forms of neolibertine eroticism is strikingly clear. Both cases manifest the prevailing Kantian figure of unsociable sociability, the emblem of market society as a disharmonic ground for individual egoisms (the *system of needs*, with Hegel's syntax). From a liberalist point of view, society springs not from the communitarian natural essence of man and from the very foundation of ethicality, but from the egoistic interest of individual competitive atoms that relate to each other in view of the greatest valorisation of their personal interest.

Similarly, from the neolibertine perspective, the ties linked to *eros* do not arise from the search for the family community as the foundation of ethical life centred on the dual unity and on the amorous synthesis obtained through the birth of children. On the contrary, they develop from the egoistic interest of individual hedonistic atoms in search of their own unlimited self-gratifying enjoyment.

As in the case of the brewer and the baker mentioned by Smith in his *Wealth of Nations*, the libertine turns to the other solely in view of the egoistic valorisation of his own interest connected with individual surplus-*jouissance*. Consequently, no less than the conduct of the liberalist, that of the libertine also violates the spirit and the letter of Kant's categorical imperative, since he employs the other as a simple means and never as an end. Love as an altruistic, giving and lastingly stable connection is dissolved in the name of individualised *jouissance*, which is by nature self-referential, egoistic, ephemeral and precarious.

The ethical community of the family is annihilated in favour of the unsociable sociability of the erotic system of needs, the new libertine-spiritual animal kingdom. In this way, the de-ethicising logic of flexibilisation, of privatisation and of atomistic individualisation of the social dimension invests the family as the foundation of ethical life: ethicised sentimental stability is replaced by the new prevailing figure of the monadic individual in permanent search of surplus-*jouissance*, without limits and with the reduction of the other to mere means of momentary pleasure always available in the unsociably sociable erotic system of needs. As in the painting *Les Amants* (1928) by René Magritte, the love relation is broken and replaced by the meeting of two self-referential solitudes, unable to even see the other before entering the relation.

Courtly love and the *dolce stil novo* give way to the imposition of immediate and uninhibited *jouissance* in the *hic et nunc*, without deferment or follow-up. The stability of love ethicised in the family bond is replaced by liquid love and by the *occasional encounter*, which becomes the emblem of flexibilisation as well as of the working and erotic-sentimental sphere. As a consequence, love itself becomes precarious and flexible, unable to root itself in the traditional ethical forms of the community of the family, which tends to be replaced by the postmodern practice of the *virtual speed date,* which impedes any possible solidification of the relation, in coherence with the physiognomy of free-market society at every level, including sentimental and interpersonal relations.

As with consumption, even in the free erotic market and in the sentimental sphere today reduced to a generalised self-service, the purpose coincides with the transition – consistent with universal flexibility – from one pleasure-commodity to another, in that search for always new relations and enjoyments – increasingly intense, uninhibited, and perverse – which, in fact, destroys the possibility of an authentic and stable relationship with the *Other*.

7

MORE ON THE ETHICAL ROOTS OF CIVIL SOCIETY

> 'Ethical powers govern the lives of individuals'.
> (Georg W. F. Hegel, *Elements of the Philosophy of Right*)

The *Sittlichkeit* also includes the sphere of education and formation. As Hegel shows in *Elements of the Philosophy of Right*, civil society must be understood as a 'universal family' (*allgemeine Familie*) permeated by ethical roots.[1]

After having accomplished the exodus from the natural family in which he saw the light, the individual 'became

1 *GPR*, § 239.

the child of civil society',[2] which must carry his burden, educating and forming him, transmitting values and principles to him.

'Initially – Hegel writes – it is the family that constitutes *the substantial Whole* (*das substantielle Ganze*) to which belongs the foresight of this particular side of the individual':[3] once the individual has become a member of the new universal family, that is, of civil society, it is up to the latter to guarantee, albeit in new form, *Vorsorge, foresight* conceived as social state. Like the family, even its major projection in the form of civil society has the task of favouring the free communitarian realisation of individualities bearers of rights and duties.

For this reason, civil society – explains Hegel – has the duty to educate its children,[4] bringing to completion the formative process already initiated by the natural family: 'civil society has the right and duty to compel parents to send their children to school',[5] so that they may become parts of civil society. For this reason, according to Hegel, there must be 'laws by which, from a certain age, children must be sent to school',[6] so that the formation initiated in the family may be further developed by the ethical roots of civil society.

2 Ibid. § 238.
3 Ibid. § 238.
4 Ibid. § 239.
5 Ibid.
6 Ibid.

On this basis, Hegel goes so far as to criticise the trend, in vogue at the time, to prematurely send children to work. It must be, once again, the ethical power of the State to protect them: 'the State has the obligation to protect children',[7] as members of the community, as children of the universal family of civil society. It must guarantee their formation and, therefore, protect them from any forces that distract them from it.

Scholastic formation managed by the ethical power of the State consequently presents itself as the delicate moment of the 'transition from the family to civil society',[8] from the particular family to the universal family. State education is tasked with the *allgemeine Bürgerbildung*, the 'formation of all as citizens',[9] as children of the universal family of civil society.

Also in this perspective, the incompatibility of the Hegelian system with the liberal tradition and, even more so, with today's neoliberal order, is strikingly clear. In this regard, it is sufficient to recall Wilhelm von Humbold's position, who, in agreement with the liberal stance, aims to limit the State and, therefore, sees as suspicious and dangerous education imposed by the State.

In a diametrically opposite way, Hegel is convinced that the school and the education of children in civil society must not be entrusted to the accidentality of individual arbitrariness and of private initiative, since

7 Ibid. § 85.

8 Hegel, *Werke in zwanzig Bänden*, X, pp. 82-83.

9 Ibid, p. 316.

they posit themselves as a fundamental *ethical condition*, as an 'essential moment in the development of the whole ethical character':[10] the school's task is precisely to favour the transition of the subject from member of the family to member of civil society, with the consequence that 'the State has the absolute duty to make sure that children receive an education',[11] through 'educational institutions accessible to all' (*allgemeine Unterrichtsanstalten*), 'comprehensive cultural formation of society' (*Gesamtbildung der Gemeine*), 'intellectual and cultural education of all'.[12] As a member of the State, the individual has the right and the duty to undergo formation, to gradually mature as a conscious and formed citizen. Through its specific ethical roots, civil society must further develop the process of ethicisation of the individual already initiated within the original family community. Civil society must also take care of the poor, guaranteeing them full rights including that of education, as members of the community and, as such, holders of imprescriptible rights: 'towards the poor, universal power takes the place of the family',[13] protecting them and treating them to all effects as their own children.

It does not comprise that otherwise noble practice that is charity, but – Hegel says – ethical *foresight* which operates 'universally',[14] guaranteeing all the members of

10 Ibid, p. 348.

11 *GPR*, § 85.

12 Hegel, *Briefe von und an Hegel* (Hamburg: Meiner, 1969-1981), II, p. 141.

13 *GPR*, § 241.

14 Ibid, § 242.

society permeated by the *ethical roots* some fundamental rights that may not be subjected to the market logics of the system of needs, that is, to the lowest level of civil society, conceived in its moment of not yet accomplished ethics.

For this reason, in Hegel's bourgeois and non-capitalistic system, the State posits itself as the guarantor of the primacy of politics over the economy, of the ethical community over isolated and egoistic individuals. Its task is to guarantee the free development of individualities within the framework of the concrete and organic community.

As 'reality of the ethical idea' (*Wirklichjkeit der sittlichen Idee*),[15] and 'reality of concrete freedom' (*Wirklichkeit der konkreten Freiheit*),[16] the State is the living ethical spirit as a substantial will, capable of realising the rights of the individual in social institutions: as the culmination of ethicality, it guarantees its active functioning through laws and political control. As Gramsci will also later recall, in Hegelian terms, 'every State is ethical because one of its most important functions is to elevate the great mass of the population to a certain cultural and moral level'.[17] The State is inevitably ethical, since it ethicises the public life of society by innervating it with the ethical roots of those intermediate entities which, from school to health, guarantee the full development of every member of the State community as a child of the universal family.

15 Ibid, § 257.

16 Ibid, § 260.

17 Gramsci, *Prison Notebooks*, VIII, § 179.

The State represents the culminating moment of ethicality, positing itself as the ultimate ethicising power *par excellence*. Through the force of a sovereign polity that is not subjected by the economy, it guarantees the vitality of the *ethical roots* of society, conceived as a *universal family* and, therefore, as the place of the free development of individualities holders of formal and material rights (civil and social) and conceived as belonging to the solidary community (as citizens with equal rights and equal duties).

The free development of the individual and the solidary community are not conceived by Hegel according to a falsely oppositional connection: they are, on the contrary, understood as complementary and in mutual correlation. In fact, the individual, as an intrinsically communitarian subject, can fully realise and develop solely within the framework of a solidary communitarian ethics, that is, in the intersubjective space permeated by the ethical roots of a society conceived as the place for the free development of all and, therefore, of the community itself as a living organism that does not exist without its parts, nor can it allow them to egoistically become autonomous by thinking themselves as antagonistic competitive atoms.

The State governs the *system of needs* and ethicises it, controlling it and preventing it from becoming autonomous, as so happens in England.[18] It permeates it through the *ethical roots* of civil society.

18 Ibid. § 245.

If the system of needs was to free itself from the ethical control of the State and its powers, what would follow would be those *tragedies in the ethical* that, through the pauperisation of the population and the concentrating of disproportionate riches in the hands of a few, would lead to the destructuring of the community and of its living *ethos*. In the name of the solidary ethical community as the space for the free and equal development of its members as children of the universal family, Hegel rejects the illuministic perspective of the system of atomistics and of the unsociably sociable fragmented society. The *sittlich* dimension is, in his view, called upon to permanently remain at the forefront, thanks to the ethicising performances of the political power of the state, so that the *animal spirits* of the autonomised economy and of the associated acquisitive individualism may not take the upper hand, generating the *tragedy in the ethical* of social polarisation and of dissolution of the communitarian fabric.

If the competitive logic of the abstract intellect applied to the social sphere should achieve hegemony, in Hegel's opinion, there could be an immediate *struggle* (*Kampf*) and an obvious *contradiction* (*Widerspruch*) between 'misery and immediately next to it the means that could put an end to it':[19] this situation, which punctually translates into the scenes of ordinary postmodernity of extreme poverty at the centre of opulent society, contains according to Hegel

19 Hegel, *Philosophie des Rechts. Die Vorlesung von 1819-20 in einer Nachschrift* (Frankfurt: Suhrkamp, 1983), p. 398.

'something revolting' (*ein Empörendes*),[20] and provokes a justified 'rebellion' (*Empörung*).[21]

Social balance must always be preserved thanks to the active intervention of State ethical power, called upon to regulate the economy and to hold it in a subordinate position with respect to politics, so that it does not cease to be at the service of the ethical community and of its members, conceived as the children of the universal family and, therefore, as such, able to benefit from imprescriptible rights and duties.

This does not mean that society resolves into a pacified desert of levelled and interchangeable individualities, as so happens within the sealed perimeters of mass homologation in the civilisation of consumption. On the contrary, the free development of individualities, even in conflictual forms, must take place within the ethicised framework of the community, where the State acts as the mediator of the parties, preventing the weaker one from being dissolved by the deregulated competitivist logic.

The social order of the *Bürgerliche Gesellschaft*, permeated by ethical roots, as Hegel conceives it, may also be described by Heraclitus' image of everlasting fire. The conflictual fire between the parts of the community alights and extinguishes according to measure, because balance is actively guaranteed by the State and by the ethical roots permeating the *Bürgerliche Gesellschaft*:

20 Hegel, *Vorlesungen über Rechtsphilosophie*, p. 342.

21 Hegel, *Philosophie des Rechts. Die Vorlesung von 1819-20 in einer Nachschrift*, p. 402.

> This *order* (κόσμον), which is identical for all things, was not created by any of the gods or by men, but always was, is and will be *everlasting fire* (πῦρ ἀείζωον), which according to *measure* (μέτρα) it sets alight and according to measure it extinguishes.[22]

As the dynamic element *par excellence*, different in all moments, but that, at the same time, always stays true to itself, Heraclitus' fire symbolises an order in motion: it stands, with unstable equilibrium, on the becoming, on a constant mediation with the conflicts and with the dissolving aspects of mercantile economy governed by the just measure of communitarian solidary ethics.

22 Hegel, *Diels-Kranz Fragmente*, 22 B 30, p. 349.

8

SERVANT AND MASTER. THE STRUGGLE FOR RECOGNITION

> 'The servant thus rises above the egoistic singularity of his natural will and so he stands above the master, who is confined to his egoism, capable of seeing in the servant only his own immediate will, recognising him in a formal manner by a consciousness that is not free'.
>
> (Georg W. F Hegel, *Encyclopedia of the Philosophical Sciences*)

The logic of the conflict should be analysed within reified society; in particular, between the eighteenth and nineteenth centuries, the capitalistic historical world produces a conflictual opposition between the proletariat. which struggles to overthrow that world because it is conscious of the contradictions that inhabit the capitalistic cosmos, as well as of its position as a 'slave class' within the mode of *Produzieren*, and the bourgeoisie, which, even though it is also part of capitalistic alienation, it tends not to oppose it, because of the material interests that it sees protected by such a system.

Each of the two opposing parties constitutes a conflictual polarity which, internal to the dynamic-contradictory totality, aspires to annihilate the other. The bourgeoisie defends its own class peculiarity, ideologically promoted as a general interest, while the proletariat fights for universal emancipation. In fact, the defence of its particularity coincides with the overcoming of the historical world of alienation and of capitalistic classism and, therefore, with the emancipation of mankind. As a result, the proletariat acts as a particular carrier for universal liberation.

The full unfolding of conflictuality corresponds, in Hegelian terms, with the dialectical figure of the Servant and Master found in the *Phenomenology of Spirit*. The bourgeoisie gives work to the proletariat and, at the same time, makes a living of such work; through the latter, the proletarian Servant attains consciousness of himself and of his condition and can act in view of the transcendence of the socio-political order. He can constitute himself as a class *an sich und für sich, in-itself and for-itself,* as a class that effectively is and knows of being so. The attainment of consciousness may only be given within the conflict, and only because of it; and this according to the idealistic theme of the identity between being and knowing, which is identified as class consciousness, so that, as highlighted by Gramsci, a worker is proletarian when he knows of being so and when he operates according to this awareness.[1]

As shown in the *Phenomenology of Spirit*, self-consciousness constitutes itself only in the dual motion by which two self-consciousnesses recognise each other as mutually recognisant. However, the single self-consciousness conceives this duplication of the self in an unequal perspective: one side is only recognised, the other is only recognisant. The servant consciousness leaves itself in the objective world and in the dimension of thingness. It finds itself among things shaped by its own reason. In this way, it forms itself (*durch die Arbeit*, 'through work',[2] Hegel writes), subjugating the object and forming it according to its own free will.

In Hegel we have, therefore, the celebration of the Servant's work against the unproductive idleness of the Master, thus overturning the entire Western tradition, which is centred on the valorisation of *otium* rather than *negotium*. Only the Servant, by working, can discipline and form himself, attaining consciousness of himself and of the world.

The real autonomous subject is now the Servant, the only one capable of acting directly, through work and

1 Gramsci, *Scritti Giovanili (1914-1918)* (Turin: Giulio Einaudi, 1958), pp. 327-328.

2 *PG*, p. 195.

in anthropising form, on the external reality and, thus, capable of forming and attaining consciousness of himself, of the objective world and of the asymmetrical relation that sees him servant. The Master, on his part, is not autonomous. His relation with the external world is mediated by the work of the Servant, on whom he depends. Devoid of a working activity, the Master lacks a real consciousness of himself and of the objective world, as well as of the real asymmetrical nature of the relation that sees him dominant.

Thus, the dialectical overturn is produced. The Servant has become the Master, and the Master has become the Servant. The truth of the process lies with the Servant, not with the Master: while the former is now free and autonomous, conscious of himself and of his relation with the objective materiality, the latter is dependent. His relation with the world of things is mediated by the work of the Servant. By fulfilling itself, servitude – Hegel explicitly writes – becomes its opposite: and it conquers only true autonomy.

If, in these pages of the *Phenomenology of Spirit*, Hegel is simply evoking a consciousness that is free because self-aware or, instead, the historical necessity of the material and revolutionary emancipation of the Servant, thus preceding Marx and Lukács, is an open question, on which there has been much debate with different outcomes and perspectives. The relation between Servant and Master – which, with Marx, will become the key for interpreting history as the theatre of class conflict – is re-addressed by Hegel in his *Encyclopedia of the Philosophical Sciences* (§ 435).

Through the working activity, the Servant comes to the elaboration of his own will and 'the transition to universal self-consciousness is achieved',[3] to the awareness of humanity as an undivided and free subject, for whom servitude, in all its forms, is a constraint worthy of being broken. From Hegel's *Encyclopedia*:

> The servant thus rises above the egoistic singularity of his natural will and so he stands above the master, who is confined to his egoism, capable of seeing in the servant only his own immediate will, recognising him in a formal manner by a consciousness that is not free. This submission of the servant's egoism constitutes the beginning of man's true freedom. The trembling of the singularity of will, the feeling of the nullity of egoism, the habit of obedience, all this is a necessary moment in the formation of humanity.[4]

Through the working activity and the progressive attainment of self-consciousness, the Servant rises above the egoistic-acquisitive individualism in which is confined the Master's consciousness, which sees in the Servant and in the surrounding world only his own will and interest.

3 *EPW*, § 435.

4 Ibid.

The overcoming of the Servant's own initial egoism, that is, his ability to relate his individual condition and his individual suffering to those of other servants, constitutes – Hegel explains – the beginning of man's true freedom as a process of liberation from all chains.

The transition from the immense power of the negative represented by the dialectics of Master and Servant is a necessary phase, as is necessary, for Hegel, its overcoming through the reversal of servitude into a true conscious autonomy. This means that, from a dialectical point of view, in which – with the *Science of Logic* – the negative is also the positive, servitude and obedience, egoism and individualism, are necessary steps for the *Bildung* of humanity as an undivided and equally free subject: hence, the consequence, explained by Marx, of the necessity to overturn the relations in which humanity is enslaved and chained, so that reason may affirm itself by fully permeating the structures of the real.

That the subjugation of the Servant must be accomplished in its negation, and therefore in the autonomy made possible by the revolution, is, indeed, one of the primary ideas that Marx draws from those pages, alongside the Hegelian discovery of labour as an anthropogenic activity and the thematisation of the historical, conflictual and dynamic processuality of alienations and disalienations by which rhythm man's self-creation is produced.

For this reason, in his *Paris Manuscripts* of 1844, Marx can bring himself to argue that the *Phenomenology of Spirit* already contains all the fundamental elements of critique, even if they are often only in embryonic form and wrapped in the mysticism of speculative lexicon.[5] What is certain is that Hegel, even beyond his intentions, is crystallising, in the pages dedicated to the relation between Servant and Master, the history of centuries, the birth and the organising of those movements that have historically given consciousness and strength to the servants spread across the planet, structuring the revolutionary action and movements for the toppling of the relation into the acquisition of true autonomy.

As well as in Marx's theoretical elaboration, which may be legitimately regarded as a further development and variation of the Hegelian Servant-Master figure, the logic of conflict and recognition outlined by Hegel also finds an efficacious visual representation in the film *The Servant* (1963), directed by Joseph Losey and scripted by Harold Pinter. The docile and meek servant who works in the Master's house, progressively gains consciousness of the situation and of the relation of power, of which the master is completely unaware. The servant gradually becomes the owner of the house in which he had initially been hired as a simple household help.

The film ends with a powerfully evocative scene: the Servant, standing stately at the top of the staircase, looks down on the Master, who is slumped on the ground at its bottom. Before the end credits, the camera moves on the clock, to underline how the process is ongoing and the

5 Diego Fusaro, *Marx Again! The Spectre Returns* (Oxford: The Pertinent Press, 2017).

overturning of the power relation is only a matter of time: in Hegelian terms, servitude will become true autonomy.

The opposition to capitalistic reification develops not only in the material sphere, with the class struggle between the bourgeoisie and the proletariat, but also in the intellectual sphere, through the genesis of the unhappy bourgeois consciousness. This latter is no other than the lacerating elaboration, by some fragments of the bourgeoisie, of the impossibility of reconciling its universal emancipatory values with the slave exploitation inherent to capitalistic classism and to the pathologies that it produces in its own image.

The bourgeoisie is configured, then, as a dialectical class, which aspires to a universal and emancipatory ethics, in line with the project of the Enlightenment; and, at the same time, it goes through the painful experience of the impossibility of implementing such an ethics due to the widespread reproduction of capital, which makes every universalistic ethics impossible, because of the slavery of labour, of colonialism and of racism.

The unhappy consciousness – of which Marx and, later, Lukács are expressions – therefore, emerges from taking the perspective of the universal at the expense of one's own particularism. The unhappy bourgeois consciousness, in search of universal emancipation, adheres to the struggles with which the Servant aims to free himself by tearing down the system of capitalistic classism and, in this way, to free humanity from universal alienation.

Therefore, capitalism and bourgeoisie are configured as two historical and conceptual determinations that do not coincide, nor are they superimposable. The former presents itself as an expressive totality that coincides with an anonymous mechanism of self-referential reproduction, nihilistically aimed at unlimited self-valorisation, with a classist relation that aims to proceed autonomously, gaining independence from the social actors who have put it into being.

As a mode of production that has today become the way of life, of desiring and of planning, capitalism is the historical classist and reified world produced by Western humanity during its historical adventure, and then – in combination with the already evoked representations of reification – no longer recognised as such, but lived as an autonomous and independent thing, as an independent and omnipotent *lord of the world*.

Magnificently expressed by the *Bildungsroman* genre, the bourgeoisie, on the other hand, corresponds to a precise dialectical subjectivity (Mozart, Hegel, Goethe and Marx are *bourgeois* but not *capitalistic* subjects), capable of developing the unhappy consciousness of the impossibility of reconciling capitalism's slave exploitation with its own universalistic emancipatory illuministic values. From the conflict between material and spiritual interests arises the unhappy consciousness of a bourgeoisie induced to reject the capitalistic contradiction and to mobilise itself, together with the proletariat, in view of a universally emancipated society.

The bourgeoisie is therefore endowed with a dialectical dual subjectivity. On the one hand, it comprises an *economic subjectivity* fully integrated with the production system, a subjectivity coinciding *tout court* with the overall strategies of capitalistic reproduction and of its nihilistic extension of the commodity form to all aspects of individual and social life. The bourgeoisie identifies itself, in Hegelian terms, with the pole of the Master who lives of servile labour and who, therefore, cannot attain consciousness of the real scission. Hence, historically, the frequent adherence of the bourgeoisie to the interests of capitalists, pure expression of the laws of capital.

On the other hand, however, the bourgeoisie presents its own irreducible emancipatory subjectivity, which tends to produce a potentially communitarian universalisation in the form of a new associated life, arising from the overcoming of pre-capitalistic limited social relations. The unhappy bourgeois consciousness is found precisely in this contrast between material reality and conscientious dimension. The particularism of a specific social position and of the material interests connected to it conflicts with the universalism of the illuministic project of emancipation and liberation.

The unhappiness of the bourgeois consciousness arises from the scission that innervates it and that, in its perennial fluctuation between particularism and universalism, prevents it from finding that immutable unity which it is also seeking. It is only by overcoming the ambiguous oscillation between these two opposite dimensions that the unhappiness of the bourgeois consciousness can, on the one hand, find the unity that it is seeking and, on the other, overcome its own particularism in the direction of universalism: it is only by adhering to the 'struggle for recognition' of the Servant's labour that, for Hegel, it 'becomes aware of the reconciliation of its own singularity with the universal'.[6]

Moreover, it is only the dialectical phenomenon of the unhappy consciousness that allows us to comprehend what pushed some, in the nineteenth and in part of the twentieth century, to embrace the *red flag* even though they did not have the material need for it. Close to the struggles for the *Anerkennung*, for the *recognition* of servile labour, the bourgeois subjectivity constitutes an element of constant instability and of weakening of capitalistic reproduction, which is forced – in Hegelian way – to look the 'negative in the face' and 'dwell with it', attaining consciousness of the fact that the contradiction of capital is capital itself.[7]

This explains, then, how the contradiction that animates the antithetic-dialectical phase is produced by the encounter of the *struggle for the recognition* of servile labour with the elaboration of the bourgeois *unhappy consciousness*, as expressed in paradigmatic way by the person, works and actions of Marx, a bourgeois anticapitalist.

6 Preve, *Storia dell'Etica* (Pistoia: Petite Plaisance, 2007), p. 311.

7 Marx, *Grundrisse*: *Foundations of the Critique of Political* Economy, trans. by M. Nicolaus (London: Penguin Books, 1973).

The *Communist Manifesto* (1848),[8] itself marks the most coherent meeting point between the material component of the *Kampf um Anerkennung* of *waged slaves* and the intellectual component of the *anglückliches Bewußtsein* of the bourgeoisie, which leaves its own particularism to adhere to the universalism of the opposite pole, that is, of the class that struggles to suppress its own servitude and that, for this reason, promotes through praxis the universal interest of overcoming the negativity of the capitalistic world.

According to young Marx's humanist lexicon, it is only with the fusion between the bourgeois 'thinking humanity' (*denkende Menschheit*) and the proletarian 'suffering humanity' (*leidende Menschheit*) that the overcoming of the contradiction infecting the present age may arise. The *dialectical phase* of the dynamics of capitalistic development therefore rests on the fusion of the two processes that can be outlined by expressions taken from the philosophical lexicon of Hegel's *Phenomenology of Spirit*: the 'struggle for recognition' (*Kampf um Anerkennung*) of the servile work of 'waged slaves' (the factory workers), and the elaboration of the 'unhappy consciousness' (*unglückliches Bewußtsein*) of that part of the bourgeoisie that, instead of adhering to the cause of the Master, it sides with the Servant and with the human universal represented by the latter's struggles.

It is the dynamic union of these two determinations that constitutes the contradiction inherent to capitalism in its dialectical phase. Thus, from the bourgeoisie, a

8 Marx and Engels, *The Communist Manifesto*.

philosophical reaction to capitalism is born, which finds its greatest expression in Fichte, Hegel and Marx, bourgeois anticapitalists. The Paris Commune, and then the Bolshevik Revolution of 1917, represent, in turn, the inflaming of the contradiction and the unfolding of the servant's strength in search for true autonomy.

It is for these reasons that, in its dialectical logic of development, capital must neutralise not only the proletariat as a conscious and revolutionary subjectivity, but also the bourgeoisie as a class that is a carrier of potential unhappy consciousness and of values that are not completely commodifiable. In other terms, in order to accomplish itself in *ab-solute* form, capital must annihilate both the bourgeois dimension of unhappy consciousness and of the world of values that are not completely commodifiable, as well as the proletarian one of oppositional consciousness and of the search for recognition of its labour.

Only in this light can we understand the morphology of today's social landscape of flexible accumulation with its post-bourgeois, post-proletarian and ultra-capitalistic order. The precariat corresponds to the new form of the dominated class, the result of the dissolution of the old bourgeoisie and of the old proletariat, now merged into an unprecedented magmatic aggregation constituting the new pole of the Servant in the historical post-1989 framework. Such a class, subordinate and without consciousness, seems to be more similar to the plebeian class outlined by Hegel in *Elements of the Philosophy of Right* than to the proletariat outlined by Marx in his *Parisian Manuscripts* of 1844. Next, we shall also reveal the identity of the new Master.

9

WITHOUT RECOGNITION. THE RETURN OF THE PLEBEIAN CLASS

'With the term *people* (*populus*) we mean the totality of men gathered in a country insofar as it constitutes a whole. That part, or the elements of it, which by common origin is recognised as being united in a civil whole, is called a *nation* (*gens*); the part that is excluded from these laws (that is, the unruly multitude of the people) is called *rabble* (*vulgus*) which, when it aggregates against the law, gives rise to a *disruptive mob* (*ager per turbas*), which excludes them from the quality of citizens.'

(I. Kant, *Anthropology from a Pragmatic Point of View*)

In *Elements of the Philosophy of Right*, Hegel focuses his attention on the genesis and composition of that highly contradictory class that is *der Pöbel, the pauperised rabble,* intended as a peculiar problem of modern society together with the division of labour, with the mass technological unemployment and with the other pathologies inherent to the capitalistic system.

Hegel is fully aware of these problems – which he conceives as an intellectualistic triumph of the system of de-ethicised needs – not only because he sees them historically realised in the England of his day, but also because he can explain them on the foundation of the same system of ethicality outlined by him, in particular in relation to the figure of atheism in the ethical world.

Since the early *Vorlesungen* on the philosophy of spirit (1803-1804/1805-1806), one of the main theoretical points, for the Stuttgart thinker, is the valorisation of the ethical communitarian moments against the atomising and intellectualistic tendencies coexisting with capitalistic modernity. In these texts preceding the *Phenomenology of Spirit*, the liberal world of wealth appears as a *savage beast* that must be tamed, controlled and dominated, so that a fruitful development of the individual and of the community can develop as an organic relation between equally free individuals.

Not subjected to the disciplinary requirements of ethicality, the market (system of needs) as the realm of 'mutual dependence' (*gegenseitiger Abhängigkeit*) is, with

Hegel, *ein wildes Tier*, 'a wild beast' that drags an ever-increasing number of individuals into the abyss of misery:

> It shifts blindly to and fro in an elementary way, and as a wild animal it needs a continuous and strict *control* (*Beherrschung*) and *taming* (*Bezähmung*).[1]

The market may well automatically restore balance to itself, as propounded by the liberal theses, but it will cast into misery, through real *tragedies in the ethical*, concrete individuals, who will lose the very right to existence. On this basis, Hegel discovers how, among the prerogatives of a system-of-needs-society that is not permeated by ethical roots, there is also, and in non-marginal way, an economic and political socialisation that physiologically generates subjectivities that are excluded from recognition (that is, they are precluded from 'being-recognised', *Anerkanntsein*), unrecognised individuals and, moreover, reproduced as irreproducible. Thus in paragraph 244 of *Elements of the Philosophy of Right*:

> The decline of a great mass below a certain standard of living, which regulates itself as the necessary standard for a member of the society in question – and with this the decline of the loss of the sentiment of right, of integrity and of the honour of providing for oneself through one's own activity and labour – gives rise to the *production of the*

1 Hegel, 'Jenenser Realphilosophie I', in *Sämtliche Werke*, ed. by Georg Lasson (Leipzig: Meiner, 1930).

plebeian mass (*Erzeugung des Pöbels*), a production which at the same time brings the capacity to more easily concentrate disproportionate riches in a few hands.[2]

The comparison between system of needs and nature heuristically finds itself again on centre stage. The system of needs is, so to speak, the nature of ethicality, since it corresponds to the negation of the ethical, to its dispersion in the atomistic system of the egoistic and competitive monads: the idea has lost itself in the pure exteriority, in the absolute fragmentation that does not know of itself and that does not even feel the need for a greater recomposition.[3] The system of needs is the *analogon* of nature because it is itself, at the social level, the apotheosis of wilderness and of lack of regulation. As written by Hegel in his Jena texts, it is a 'wild beast' and undisciplined. Consequently, the single subjectivity at the mercy of the *status naturae* of the system of needs is necessarily subjected to the uncertainty, the insecurity and the perennial conflictuality of the market: the market that is not permeated by ethical roots appears as a wilderness comparable to a natural environment that has not been anthropised by human activity. There is no guarantee that he may really satisfy his needs and the only existing rule is the *bellum omnium contra omnes* of individualistic competitivism.

For this reason, in Hegel's view, Hobbes' *status naturae* corresponds to the system of needs as the realm of wild

2 *GPR*, § 244.

3 Paul Chamley, *Économie Politique et Philosophie chez Steuart et Hegel* (Paris: Dalloz, 1963).

nature at the social level. If, however, for Hobbes, the state of nature coincides with the natural-eternal condition of man, which may only be controlled through the State and its figures, for Hegel, it is to be understood as an area of temporary eclipsing of the ethical element, but also as a temporary fall that needs to be overcome through the reinstatement of the original ethical element of the family brought to a higher level.

Following an ideological naturalisation of the modern capitalistic condition, Hobbes is convinced that the state of nature realises man's natural unsociability; whereas for Hegel it stands as the negation of the human being's original communitarian character, supported by the family as an immediate community established on feelings.

In the sphere of the system of needs, there no longer is the immediate and particular ethicality of the family: instead, what prevails is 'the empirical infinity of singularities' in conflict, agonal, competitive, suspicious and unsociably sociable.[4] It is, as Hegel says, the 'state of the merchants', who hold 'the absolute mistrust' towards the universal.[5] Indeed, for the merchant, *to value* means *to have*: with the consequence that universal interest is deprived of quality and replaced by mere quantity. In the triumph of *total competitive ruthlessness*,[6] everything is sacrificed on the altar of profit as the only recognised universal: the I of the society of merchants can thus universalise itself only

4 Hegel, *The Jena Lectures on the Philosophy of Spirit*.

5 Ibid.

6 Ibid.

through the mediation of the market, the circulation of money, the exchange system.

Far from realising himself, as the liberal rhetoric chants, the individual dispersed in the individualistic system of non-sociable society loses himself in the fragmentation and in a dimension that, by negating the communitarian character of the human being, it impedes the full realisation of society as well as of the individuals that inhabit it: the anomic individualism annihilates the individual, who loses himself, exposed as he is to the disjoining power of the un-ethicised economy and to the 'blind dependence' (*blinding Abhängigkeit*) that it produces.[7]

As a product of the de-ethicised system of needs, the plebeian mass appears as the aggregation of the excluded and of the unrecognised, generated by the tragedies in the ethical of the deregulated system of needs devoid of any ethical element. It can be legitimately defined as the corporation of the malcontent, populated by those who are not part of those 'corporations' of civil society through which they could have attained their dignity as social beings.

If, as Hegel shows with the subsequent figures of the *bürgerliche Gesellschaft*, or *civil society*, the corporation corresponds, in essence, to the incarnation of the universal into the particular through labour as the necessary mediation for social recognition, then it follows that the plebeian mass as a corporation of the corporation-less, is

7 Ibid.

ab intrinseco denied of the recognition that is socially and politically valid in the spheres of the State.

Central to paragraphs 240 and 241 of the *Rechtsphilosophie, der Pöbel* (*the plebeian mass, rabble*), does not purely coincide with *poverty* (*Armut*). It is, more precisely, poverty with the 'sentiment of its injustice' (*Gefühl ihres Unrechts*). Such a sentiment is generated from the fact that the plebeian mass as the corporation of the corporation-less finds its in-itselfness and, at least in part, a glimpse of for-itselfness in knowing itself to be paradoxically excluded from ethicality: it does not benefit from ethical roots and it is subject to the processes of exclusion caused by the deregulated course of the system of needs deprived of the elements of ethicality.

Armut and *Pöbel*, *poverty* and *plebeian mass*, are never used synonymously in Hegel's texts. The plebeian mass is characterised by poverty combined with the awareness and the sense of injustice with respect to a situation perceived, albeit in a conceptually non-systematised form, as unjust:

> Poverty in itself does not make the plebeian mass: this is determined only by the disposition associated with poverty, by inward rebellion against the rich, against society, government and so on.[8]

On this point, especially in relation to the English situation ('these phenomena can be studied on a large scale in the example of England', *Elements of the Philosophy of*

8 *GPR*, § 244.

Right, § 245), Hegel insists on associating the genesis of the plebeian mass with the de-ethicisation of the system of needs as a moment of the abstract intellect that has disjointed the totality and has allowed the system of competitive atomistics to prevail. There are accidental circumstances that:

> can reduce individuals to poverty, to a situation which leaves them with the needs of civil society, and which, [...] makes them more or less deprived of all the advantages of society, of the ability to acquire skills and education in general, even in the administration of justice, health care, and often even of the comfort of religion.[9]

The plebeian mass, therefore, is located in the system of needs that generated it and, at the same time, it is excluded from it, since it lacks the necessary means (money in particular) to be able to benefit from recognition: money which is, in the system of needs, the only possible form of the *Anerkennung*.[10] For this reason, the plebeian mass is deprived of the 'advantages of society', among which Hegel mostly identifies culture, justice and health.

In fact, the exclusion to which it is condemned translates into a loss of citizenship, if by citizenship we mean both

9 Ibid, § 241.

10 On the theme of *Anerkennung* see Ludwig Siep, *Anerkennung als Prinzip der praktischen Philosophie. Untersuchungen zu Hegels Jenaer Philosophie des Geistes* (Freiburg: Alber, 1979) and Robert R. Williams, *Hegel's Ethics of Recognition* (London: University of California Press, 1997); Robert R. Williams, *Recognition. Fichte and Hegel on the Other* (Albany: State University of New York, 1992).

active participation to national political life, as well as to the use of services and rights which, in the system of ethicality, should *naturaliter* be granted in the form of rights to every member of the *universal family* through to the intervention of the ethicising power of the State. So even for Hegel, as for Kant in *Pragmatic Anthropology*, the plebeian mass may be identified with that part of the nation that is 'excluded from the status of State citizenship'.

In short, *disjointment* (*Zerrissenheit*), *deprivation and necessity* (*Entbehrung und Not*) constitute, from Hegel's point of view, the salient traits of the plebeian mass. Moreover, it lacks its own specific language, its own coherent vision of the world. It is only endowed with the sentiment of wrong, which is vague and generic, but it is not able to articulate it conceptually, nor to transform it into a redemptive political project. Endowed with an opaque, unconscious and subterranean subjectivity, the plebeian mass thus ends up speaking the same language of the classes recognised in the system of needs and, therefore, accepting the narratives that contemplate the very exclusion of the plebeian mass. The latter is, therefore, a dominated and subaltern class.

In *Elements of the Philosophy of Right*, Hegel highlights how the plebeian mass, as well as of language, of consciousness and of recognition, is also deprived of existential stability. Free from the protection connected to the system of ethicality, exposed to the wavering movements of the market and of its unfathomable dynamics, it is forced into an insecure existence devoid of certainties. Its very existence is not guaranteed in consolidated forms and, consequently, it is forced to fluctuate without ethical roots and to never assume the forms of the mature stability given by the family, by employment, by health, by education and by the active participation in politics. Hegel writes:

> If the individual is not a member of a legally authorised corporation (and it is only through legal recognition that a common thing becomes a corporation), he is without the *honour of belonging to an estate*, in his isolation he is reduced to the egoistic side of his trade, his subsistence and his satisfaction *lack stability* (*nichts Stehendes*).[11]

According to Pasquale Salvucci,[12] the figure of the plebeian mass in Hegel's system of ethicality entirely corresponds to Marx's proletariat. They are identical both in their social and economic genesis as an excluded and exploited mass, and in their revolutionary political significance destined to bring down the system of needs or the capitalistic mode of production.

However, beyond the analogies and the isomorphisms, the differences between the Hegelian plebeian mass and the Marxian proletariat are strikingly clear and allow,

11 *GPR*, § 253.

12 Pasquale Salvucci, *Lezioni sulla Hegeliana Flosofia del Diritto. La Società Civile* (Milan: Guerini, 2000).

perspectively, to decipher the essence of precarity. This latter seems structurally, in its current condition, to be much closer to Hegel's plebeians than to Marx's proletariat.

The new postmodern, post-bourgeois, post-proletarian, precarious-plebeian mass, lacks a class language and consciousness, it generically perceives the injustice connected to its endemic misery, it is forced into flexible, precarious and unsecure existential forms, it is increasingly excluded from citizenship. As the successor to Marx's proletariat, the precarious class appears as an unspeakable return of Hegel's plebeian mass in the horizon of the new system of needs de-ethicised on a planetary scale.

It is certainly true that even Hegel's plebeian mass may be open to certain revolutionary tendencies, such as when it smashes machines up in England and when it acquires political initiatives as in France. And yet, the absence of political organisation and of class consciousness clearly distinguishes it from the Marxian proletariat, the *old mole* that consciously works underground and suddenly appears for transcending the social world that determines its oppression. There is a passage in the *Rechtsphilosophie* which could in all effect be a class photograph of the new precarious-plebeian Servant inherent to the flexible accumulation of capital:

> The many, as the single, which may be favourably intended as *the people*, certainly live together, but only as a *multitude* (*Menge*) – a *shapeless mass* (*formlose Masse*), whose movement and activity would therefore

> only be elemental, irrational, beastly and terrifying.[13]

It is also interesting to note how the concept of proletariat is almost absent in Hegel's reflection (if by proletariat we mean, in a Marxian sense, the class in-itself and for-itself of workers subjected to the extortion of surplus labour), just as the plebeian aspect is not specifically dealt with by Marx and is not even found in the pages devoted to the commentary on Hegel's political philosophy in *Critique of Hegel's Philosophy of Right*; the latter aspect being decidedly enigmatic if we consider that in this Marxian text the most profound element regarding the Hegelian analysis is explicitly identified with the observation that the separation of civil society and political society is a contradiction.

More precisely, Hegel focuses on the exploitation in the factory linked to the practices of the division of labour without, however, outlining the new figure of the proletariat in-itself and for-itself. For Hegel, the system of exploitation and of the *wild beast* of de-ethicised market connected to the big industry does not produce a revolutionary class, but a mass of desperate people, a plebeian mass without consciousness, without a language and without stability, abandoned to misery and impossible to redeem itself:

> A number of people are therefore condemned to factory and manufacturing jobs [...] that completely obtund [...], and branches of industry that gave life to a

13 *GPR*, § 303.

> large class of men suddenly dry out due to trends or to the decrease in prices following inventions [made] in other countries, and so on, and *all these people are abandoned to misery* (*diese ganze Menge ist der Armuth*), to which they can in no way find remedy.[14]

Similarly, Marx, especially in the pages of *Das Kapital* dedicated to *primitive accumulation*, outlines the profile of the plebeian mass generated by the new mode of production in its abstract phase, centred on expropriation and on the forced creation of excluded masses. But it is especially in relation to the genesis of the proletariat as a class in- and for-itself, that his analysis takes place. From a certain perspective, it is as if Hegel could not yet see the proletariat, while Marx could no longer see the plebeian mass, in so far as it represents, for the Trier philosopher, the new figure of the proletariat.

With the current triumph of post-bourgeois and post-proletarian flexible capitalism, we are witnessing the overwhelming return of the plebeian mass on the social and economic scene. Absolute capitalism has *aufgehoben*, *overcome*, its own contradiction of the dialectical phase, represented mainly by the bourgeois and proletarian classes, and has now repolarised society in an unprecedented form: on one side, the restricted circle of financial aristocracy embodied by the speculative *merchants* of the de-ethicised system of needs; on the other, the new plebeian multitude that has incorporated the two preceding classes of the

14 Hegel, *The Jena Lectures on the Philosophy of Spirit*.

proletariat and of the bourgeoisie and that lacks stability, a shared language, a consciousness and an organised conflictual capacity.

Capitalism, which, in its abstract phase, had produced the plebeian class, now generates it again in the absolute phase as the dissolution of the proletariat and of the bourgeoisie and as the fragmentation of the old ethical elements that still bound and tamed the *wild beast* of the system of needs.

Thus, Hegel's words of return to the ethical, welcomingly resound as a distant echo in our time of de-politicisation and de-ethicisation: in the society of ethical roots and of regulated market *kein Pöbel entstehen soll, no plebeian mass must form* (*Elements of the Philosophy of Right*, § 244). Everyone has the right and duty to exist as an equally free citizen in the spaces of ethical community as his universal family.

Today's precariat is the new class emerging from the ashes of the proletariat as an immense pole of the dominated in the post-modern age, perhaps more similar, at least in this phase, to the *plebeian mass* of the de-ethicised system of needs described by Hegel than to the proletariat in-itself and for-itself outlined by Marx.

In the new landscape of class conflict that has been taking shape since 1989, bi-classism survives while biunivocal conflict has disappeared: exploitation survives, while the struggle against it has been neutralised. Classist inequality increases, while the struggle aimed at overcoming it has been put aside. The pole of the Master attacks, while that of the Servant does not even defend itself anymore. The antagonistic and solidary consciousness of the proletariat in search of better futures has dissolved into the resigned and individualistic unconsciousness of the precariat as an amorphous plebeian mass composed of serial and resigned solitudes. The proletariat perceived itself as a cohesive class endowed with in-itselfness and for-itselfness, and on this basis it modulated its own activity. On its part, the precariat is currently composed of a shapeless, competitive and incommunicative mass of individual homologues that, in-itself but not for-itself, appear as mere atoms supplying a flexible, underpaid and increasingly less safeguarded labour-force.

It is necessary to insist on this point: the precarisation of labour, coyly defined *flexibility*, places itself in the very hands of the Master as an instrument of class conflict. The dominated are today reduced to amorphous material at the mercy of the logics of valorisation, to a postmodern, post-bourgeois and post-proletarian plebeian mass, freed from the elements of bourgeois ethicality (State, family, Hegelian *ethical roots* and public bodies), and from the dimension of proletarian safeguards (social rights, trade union protection etc.), and of class consciousness. In-itself but not for-itself, the new precarious-plebeian Servant is a disarmed and individualised subject, without consciousness or antagonistic polity, devoid of an alternative world vision in the name of which to operationally endure what Lukács defined the 'terrible and definitive narrative of dominant capitalism'.[15]

For this reason, the new oligarchs of the post-1989 world order emphatically insist that class struggle is over and that, therefore, it is time to universally cooperate with the economy so that, abandoned to its course, it may produce generalised well-being, according to the reiterated Smithsonian theorem of the *invisible hand*.[16] The new post-bourgeois and ultra-capitalistic Master, having temporarily won the war, aspires to eternalise the dominant order that is in his favour and, therefore, to induce the new plebeian Servant to accept it remissibly.

The transition from the proletariat to the precariat may be understood in this light and on this foundation, as the consistent development of the conflict between Servant and Master, in the sense not of its suppression, but of its reconfiguration entirely to the benefit of the Master, according to a form such that the relation of classist power may survive, if not intensify, and, together, allowing the destructuring of the organisational and opposing capacity of the Servant. The forms of flexibility, far from being intrinsically neutral, favour the weakening of the Servant and the strengthening of the Master. The former becomes pauperised plebeian, the latter becomes financial aristocracy. Exploitation and inequality intensify

15 Lukács, *The Young Hegel*.

16 Maryse Bresson, *Sociologie de la Précarité* (Paris: Colin, 2007).

as never before and, at the same time, the oppositional and conflictual capacity of the Servant is dissolved.

We know that, historically, the biunivocal social conflictuality between Servant and Master has always tended to extend both the sphere of social rights and the political participation of the masses. It is the defining character of the development of capitalism in its historical adventure in the dialectical phase: the Master grants only what the Servant, in his struggle (*in dem Kampf*), forces him to grant. Labour does not obtain safeguards and guarantees except those that, through the practices of the conflict, it seizes from capital.

Without being confronted by the opposite pole of resistance, struggle and protests, capital and the Master would take everything, including the bare life of the worker. It is only in the conscious class conflict that capital can be opposed, limited and finally demolished. The economic contradiction is politically removed through the planned agency of the Servant, who is organised as a class and as a party: in Gramsci's words, 'the economic contradiction becomes political contradiction and is politically resolved in the overturning of praxis', by the organised and conscious subjectivity.

Among the paradoxical traits of today's post-1989 landscape, there is also the redeployment, in an unprecedented form, of the conflict between Servant and Master. The reforms, the protests and the revolts are, as absurd as it may seem, concocted and executed by the Master himself. The latter, in our time of defunct historical communism, in the decomposition of the world of working activity and of the Servant's oppositional consciousness, aspires to redefine the power relation not to extend rights and to favour inclusion, but for the opposite objective. The fragmentation of labour and the financialisation of the economy are the two levers of the reaction of capital to the struggle of the worker.[17]

In order to affirm itself in absolute form, capital dissolves the class in-itself and for-itself of the proletariat, redefined as a passive plebeian mass, fragmenting it both at the level of the real and of the symbolic; and, in synergistic way, it favours the financialisation of the economy, that is, its increasingly marked independence from the direct mediation of human labour and from the traditional enterprise. For this reason, the so-called 'necessary structural reforms' invoked and implemented in Europe today almost always coincide with a neoliberal reorganisation of the working world that exclusively benefits the post-bourgeois and post-proletarian globalist Master. The incontrovertible proof of this resides in the punctual and pauperising outcomes of the aforementioned *reforms*.

These so-called *reforms* are characterised by the removal of rights and by the increasingly massive deregulation of the de-politicised and de-ethicised economy, but also by the complete privatisation and the devastation of the constitutional structure inspired by the welfare state and by communitarian solidarity. The *reforms* promoted by the

17 Gramsci, *Prison Notebooks*, X, p. 33.

Masters of globalisation in their own interest, correspond, therefore, if observed from the Servant's perspective, to de-emancipating counter-reforms. They destroy what is left of the social state, they spread and accentuate precarity and insecurity, they always generate new tragedies in the ethical. They attack the working world and the social achievements conquered by the politically organised Servant. What prevails at every latitude, is Castel's expression of *insécurité social*,[18] typical of the society of risk and of integral precarity.

If capitalistic society rests on class conflict, this latter also affects the categories of thought: just as the interests of one pole are opposite to those of the other, so are the conceptual categories of a part, in theory, incompatible with those of the other. The material class struggle always proceeds next to the cultural class struggle. The *reforms* – to mention only one example – with which the neo-oligarchic Master is eroding the rights of the new plebeian Servant and decomposing the working world, are such only for the dominant pole: for the dominated, instead, they correspond to as many *counter-reforms* that, as such, should be strongly rejected.

18 Robert Castel, *L'insécurité Sociale. Qu'est-ce qu'Être Protége?* (Paris: Seuil, 2003).

BIBLIOGRAPHY

Adorno, Theodor W. and Max Horkheimer, *Dialectic of Enlightenment* (New York: Verso, 2016)

Adorno, Theodor W., *Minima Moralia. Reflections on a Damaged Life*, trans. by E. F. N. Jephcott (London: Verso, 2005)

Alessio, Manuela, *Azione ed Eticità in Hegel. Saggio sulla 'Filosofia del Diritto'* (Milan: Guerini, 1996)

Aristotle, *Metaphysics* (Indianapolis: Hackett, 2016)

----------- *Nicomachean Ethics* (London: University of Chicago Press, 2012)

----------- *Politics* (Newburyport: Focus Pub., 2012)

Attali, Jacques, *Karl Marx, ou l'Esprit du Monde* (Paris: Fayard, 2005)

Bauer, Christoph Johannes, *Das Geheimnis aller Bewegung ist ihr Zweck. Geschichtsphilosophie bei Hegel und Droysen* (Hamburg: Felix Meiner Verlag, 2001)

Bauman, Zygmunt, *Liquid Love. On the Frailty of Human Bonds* (Oxford: Blackwell, 2003)

Benoist, Alain de, 'On Identity', *Telos* 128 (2004), 9-64

Berman, Marshall, *All That is Solid Melts Into Air. The Experience of Modernity* (New York: Simon and Schuster, 1982)

Bobbio, Norberto, *Studi Hegeliani* (Turin: Einaudi, 1982)

Bockenheimer, Eva, *Hegels Familien- und Gechlechtertheorie* (Hamburg: Meiner, 2013)

Bourgeois, Bernard, *La Pensée Politique de Hegel* (Paris: PUF, 1969)

Bouton, Christophe, *Temps et Esprit dans la Philosophie de Hegel: De Francfort à Iéna* (Paris: Vrin, 2000)

Bresson, Maryse, *Sociologie de la Précarité* (Paris: Colin, 2007)

Castel, Robert, *L'insécurité Sociale. Qu'est-ce qu'Être Protége?* (Paris: Seuil, 2003)

Cerroni, Umberto, *Societa Civile e Stato Politico in Hegel* (Bari: De Donato, 1974)

Cesa, Claudio (ed.), *Il pensiero politico di Hegel* (Rome: Laterza, 1979)

Cesa, Claudio, *Stato e Libertà negli Scritti Politici di Hegel* (Florence: Olschki, 1971)

Chamley, Paul, *Économie Politique et Philosophie chez Steuart et Hegel* (Paris: Dalloz, 1963)

Chavance, Bernard, *Marx et le Capitalisme. La Dialectique d'un Système* (Paris: Nathan, 1996)

Clark, Maurice, *Logic and System. A Study of the Transition from "Vorstellung" to Thought in the Philosophy of Hegel* (Hague: Nijhoff, 1971)

Cornehl, Peter, *Die Zukunft der Versöhnung: Eschatologie und Emanzipation in der Aufklärung, bei Hegel und in der Hegelschen Schule* (Göttingen: Vandenhoeck & Ruprecht, 1971)

Cortella, Lucio, *L'Etica della Democrazia. Attualità della Filosofia del Diritto di Hegel* (Genova: Marietti, 2011)

Curi, Umberto (ed.), *Società Civile e Stato fra Hegel e Marx* (Padova: CLESP, 1980)

D'Hondt, Jacques (ed.), *Hegel et le siècle des Lumières* (Paris: Presses universitaires de France, 1974)
D'Hondt, Jacques, 'Hegel e il Socialismo Nascente', in *Rivista di Filosofia* (1977)
---------------------- *Hegel Secret: Recherches sur les Sources Cachées de la Pensée de Hegel* (Paris: PUF, 1968)
Deleuze, Giles, *Rhizome* (Paris: Minuit, 1976)
Derrida, Jacques, *Spectres of Marx* (New York: Routledge, 1994)
Durkheim, Emile, *The Rules of Sociological Method* (New York: Free Press, 1982)

Fichte, Johann Gottlieb, *Sämmtliche Werke*, III (Berlin: De Gruyter, 1965)
Fraser, Ian, *Hegel and Marx. The Concept of Need* (Edinburgh: Edinburgh University Press, 1998)
Fusaro, Diego, *Marx Again! The Spectre Returns* (Oxford: The Pertinent Press, 2017)

Gramsci, Antonio, *Prison Notebooks* (New York: Columbia University Press, 2011)
--------------------- *Scritti Giovanili (1914-1918)* (Turin: Giulio Einaudi, 1958)
Günter Rohtmoser, *Théologie e Aliénation dans la Pensée du Jeune Hegel* (Paris: Beauchesne, 1970)

Habermas, Jürgen, *Kleine politische Schriften (I-IV)* (Frankfurt: Suhrkamp 1980)
----------------------- *The Philosophical Discourse of Modernity* (Cambridge: MIT Press, 1987)

Hartkopf, William, 'Die Dialektik Fichtes als Vorstufe zu Hegels Dialektik', *Zeitschrift für philosophische Forschung*, 21.2 (1967), 173-207

Hegel, Georg Wilhelm Friedrich, *Aesthetics. Lectures on Fine Arts*, trans. by T. M. Knox (Oxford: Clarendon Press, 1975)

-- *Briefe von und an Hegel* (Hamburg: Meiner, 1969-1981)

-- *Die Vernunft in der Geschichte* (Meiner, 1917)

-- *Elements of the Philosophy of Right*, trans. by H. B. Nisbet (Cambridge: Cambridge University Press, 1991)

-- *Encyclopedia of the Philosophical Sciences*, trans. by A.V. Miller (Oxford: Oxford University Press, 1990)

-- *Fragmente über Volksreligion und Christentum* (1794)

-- *Gesammelte Werke*, VIII (Hamburg: Meiner, 1976)

-- *Gesammelte Werke*, VIII, ed. by R. P. Horstmann and J. H. Trede (Hamburg: Meiner, 1976)

-- *Grundlinien der Philosophie des Rechts,* trans. by H.B. Nisbet, Elements of the Philosophy of Right (Cambridge: Cambridge University Press, 1991)

-- *Hegels theologische Jugendschriften* (Heidelberg: Tübingen, J.C.B. Mohr, 1907)

-------------------------------------- *Jenenser Realphilosophie I*, in *Sämtliche Werke* XIX (Leipzig: Meiner, 1913)

-------------------------------------- *Lectures on the Philosophy of Religion*, ed. by P. C. Hodgson (Berkeley: University of California Press, 1988)

-------------------------------------- *Phänomenologie des Geistes*, trans. by A. V. Miller (Oxford: Oxford University Press, 1977)

-------------------------------------- *Philosophie des Rechts. Die Vorlesung von 1819-20 in einer Nachschrift* (Frankfurt: Suhrkamp, 1983)

-------------------------------------- *Philosophy of Mind*, trans. by W. Wallace and A. V. Miller (Oxford: Clarendon Press, 2007)

-------------------------------------- *Sämtliche Werke* XIX (Leipzig: Meiner, 1913)

-------------------------------------- *Schriften und Entwürfe (1799-1808)* (Leipzig: Meiner, 1998)

-------------------------------------- *Suhrkamp-Werkausgabe* 2 (Frankfurt: Suhrkamp, 1979)

-------------------------------------- *The Jena Lectures on the Philosophy of Spirit* (Detroit: Wayne State University Press, 1983)

-------------------------------------- *The Phenomenology of Spirit*, trans. by A. V. Miller (Oxford: Oxford University Press, 1977)

-------------------------------------- *The Philosophy of History*, trans. by J. Sibree (New York: Dover Publications, 2004)

-------------------------------------- *The Science of Logic*, trans. by G. Di Giovanni, (Cambridge: Cambridge

University Press, 2010)

------------------------------------- *Theologische Jugendschriften*, ed. by H. Nohl, (Frankfurt: Minerva, 1996)

------------------------------------- *Natural law: the scientific ways of treating natural law, its place in moral philosophy, and its relation to the positive sciences of law* (Philadelphia: University of Pennsylvania Press, 1975)

------------------------------------- *Vorlesungen über die Philosophie der Geschichte* (Frankfurt: Suhrkamp, 1970)

------------------------------------- *Vorlesungen über die Philosophie der Religion, 1821-1831* (California: University of California Press, 1988)

------------------------------------- *Vorlesungen über Rechtsphilosophie 1818-1831*, ed. by K.-H. Ilting (Stuttgart: Frommann, 1973-1974)

------------------------------------- *Werke in zwanzig Bänden* (Stuttgart: Frommann, 1969-1979)

------------------------------------- *Werke*, trans. by E. S. Haldane (London: Kegan Paul, Trench, Trübner & Co, 1892)

------------------------------------- *Wissenschaft der Logik*, trans. by G. Di Giovanni (Cambridge: Cambridge University Press, 2010)

Heidegger, Martin, *Being and Time*, trans. by J. Stambaugh (Albany: State University of New York Press, 1996)

Heine, Felix, *Freiheit und Totalität. Zum Verhältnis von Philosophie und Wirklichkeit bei Fichte und Hegel* (Bonn:

Bouvier, 1980)

Hinchman, Lewis P., *Hegel's Critique of the Enlightenment* (Gainesville: University Presses of Florida, 1984)

Honneth, Axel, *Leiden an Unbestimmtheit: Eine Reaktualisierung der Hegelschen Rechtsphilosophie* (Stuttgart: Reclam, 2001)

Hume, David, *A Treatise of Human Nature* (New York: Fordham University Press, 1995)

Husserl, Edmund, *Teleologie in der Philosophiegeschichte* (1936)

Hyppolite, Jean, *Genesis and Structure of Hegel's Phenomenology of Spirit* (Evanston: Northwestern University Press, 1947)

Ilting, Karl-Heinz, *Aufsätze über Hegel* (Frankfurt: Humanities Online, 2006)

Kaltenbrunner, Gerd-Klaus, *Hegel und die Folgen* (Freiburg: Rombach, 1970)

Kant, Immanuel, *On History,* trans. by Lewis White Beck (New Jersey: Prentice Hall, 2001)

Koselleck, Reinhart, et al. *Geschichtliche Grundbegriffe* (Stuttgart: Klett-Cotta, 2004)

Krings, Hermann, *Die Entfremdung zwischen Schelling und Hegel: 1801-1807* (München: Bayerische Akademie der Wissenschaft, 1977)

Kunzli, Arnold, *Aufklärung und Dialektik: politische Philosophie von Hobbes bis Adorno* (Freiburg: Rombach, 1971)

Lamb, David (ed.), *Hegel and Modern Philosophy* (London: Croom Helm, 1987)

Landucci, Sergio, *Hegel: la Coscienza e la Storia. Approssimazione alla 'Fenomenologia dello Spirito'* (Florence: La Nuova Italia, 1976)

Lebre, Jérôme, *Hegel à l'Épreuve de la Philosophie Contemporaine: Deleuze, Lyotard, Derrida* (Paris: Ellipses, 2002)

Lefebvre, Jean-Pierre and Pierre Macherey, *Hegel et la Société* (Paris: PUF, 2016)

Locke, John, *Second Treatise of Government* (New York: John Wiley & Sons, 2014)

Lonzi, Carla, *Sputiamo su Hegel* (Rome: Editoriale Grafica, 1970)

Löwith, Karl, *From Hegel to Nietzsche: The Revolution in 19th Century Thought* (New York: Constable & Co., 1965)

--------------- *Max Weber and Karl Marx* (London: Routledge, 2002)

Lukács, György, *The Destruction of Reason Die Zerstörung der Vernunft*, trans. by P. R. Palmer (London: Merlin, 1980)

Lukács, György, *The Destruction of Reason Die Zerstörung der Vernunft*, trans. by P.R. Palmer (London: Merlin, 1980)

Lukács, György, *The Ontology of Social Being* (London: Merlin, 1980)

Lukács, György, *The Young Hegel* (London: Merlin, 1975)

MacGregor, David, *Hegel, Marx and the English State* (Boulder: Westview, 1992)

Mancina, Claudia, *Differenze nell'Eticità: Amore, Famiglia, Società Civile in Hegel* (Naples: Guida, 1991)

Marcuse, Herbert, *Hegel's Ontology and the Theory of Historicity*, trans. by S. Benhabib (Cambridge: MIT Press, 1987)

---------------------- *One-Dimensional Man. Studies in the Ideology of Advanced Industrial Society* (Boston: Beacon Press, 1964)

---------------------- *Reason and Revolution. Hegel and the Rise of Social Theory* (Oxford: Oxford University Press, 1941)

Marion, Jean-Luc, *Being Given: Toward a Phenomenology of Givenness* (Stanford: Stanford University Press, 2002)

Marx, Karl and Friedrich Engels, *The Communist Manifesto* (London: Penguin Classics, 2014)

Marx, Karl, *Capital. A Critique of Political Economy*, trans. by B. Fowkes (London: Penguin Classics, 1990)

------------- *Early Writings* (New York: Penguin, 1992)

------------- *Grundrisse: Foundations of the Critique of Political Economy*, trans. by M. Nicolaus (London: Penguin Books, 1973)

Masullo, Aldo, *La Potenza della Scissione* (Naples: Edizioni scientifiche italiane, 1997)

McCarney, Joseph, *Hegel on History* (New York: Routledge, 2000)

Merleau-Ponty, Maurice, *Sense and Non-sense* (Evanston:

Northwestern University Press, 1964)

Monaldi, Marcello, *Hegel e la Storia. Nuove Prospettive e Vecchie Questioni* (Naples: Guida, 2000)

Ottman, Henning, *Individuum und Gemeinschaft bei Hegel*, I, *Hegel im Spiegel der Interpretationen* (Berlin: De Gruyter, 1977)

Paperzak, Adriaan, *Philosophy and Politics. A Commentary on the Preface to Hegel's Philosophy of Right* (Dordrecht: Springer, 1987)

Papi, Fulvio, *Lezioni sulla 'Scienza della Logica' di Hegel* (Milano: Ghibli, 2000)

Pascale, Carla De (ed.), *Fichte und die Aufklärung* (Hildesheim: Olms, 2004)

Pasolini, Pier Paolo, *Saggi sulla Politica e la Società* (Milan: Mondadori 2016)

Patten, Alan, *Hegel's Idea of Freedom* (Oxford: Oxford University Press, 1999)

Pełczyński, Zbigniew, *Hegel's Political Philosophy. Problems and Perspectives* (Cambridge: Cambridge University Press, 1971)

Petyx, Vincenza, *Dimenticare la Rivoluzione: la Cultura di Destra nella Francia di Fine Ottocento* (Naples: La Città del Sole, 1995)

------------------ *I Selvaggi in Europa: la Francia Rivoluzionaria di Maistre e Bonald* (Napoli: Bibliopolis 1988)

Pinkard, Terry, *Hegel's Phenomenology. The Sociality of Reason* (Cambridge: Cambridge University Press,

1994)

Pippin, Robert B. and Otfried Höffe, *Hegel on Ethics and Politics* (Cambridge: Cambridge University Press, 2004)

Plato, *Republic* (London: Penguin, 2012)

------ *The Dialogues of Plato* (New Haven: Yale University Press, 1984)

Popper, Karl R., *The Open Society and Its Enemies* (London: Routledge, 1945)

Preve, Costanzo, *Elogio del Comunitarismo* (Napoli: Controcorrente, 2006)

------------------- *Hegel Antiutilitarista* (Rome: Settimo Sigillo, 2007)

------------------- *La Quarta Guerra Mondiale* (Parma: Insegna del Veltro, 2008)

------------------- *Storia dell'Etica* (Pistoia: Petite Plaisance, 2007)

------------------- *Storia della Dialettica* (Pistoia: Petite Plaisance, 2006)

Racinaro, Roberto and Vincenzo Vitiello, *Logica e Storia in Hegel* (Rome: Edizioni Scientifiche Italiane, 1985)

Rametta, Gaetano, *Il Concetto del Tempo: Eternità e Darstellung Speculativa nel Pensiero di Hegel* (Milan: Angeli, 1989)

Riley, Patrick, *Will and Political Legitimacy. A Critical Exposition of Social Contract Theory in Hobbes, Locke, Rousseau, Kant, and Hegel* (Jan Jose: ToExcel, 1999)

Ritter, Joachim, *Hegel and the French Revolution* (Cambridge: MIT Press, 1984)

------------------- *Metaphysik und Politik. Studien zu Aristoteles und Hegel* (Frankfurt: Suhrkamp, 1969)

Rizzi, Lino, *Eticità e Stato in Hegel* (Milan: Mursia, 1993)

Rohtmoser, Günter, *Théologie e Aliénation dans la Pensée du Jeune Hegel* (Paris: Beauchesne, 1970)

Röpke, Wilhelm, *The Social Crisis of our Time* (London: Transaction Publishers, 2009)

Rorty, Richard, *Philosophy and the Mirror of Nature* (Princeton: Princeton University Press, 1979)

Rosanvallon, Pierre, *Le Capitalisme Utopique* (Paris: Seuil, 1979)

Rosenzweig, Franz, *Hegel und der Staat* (Berlin: Suhrkamp, 2010)

Rosinger, Margery, *Die Einheit von Ethik und Ontologie bei Hegel* (Frankfurt: Lang, 1980)

Rossi, Mario, *Marx e la Dialettica Hegeliana. I, Hegel e lo Stato* (Rome: Editori Riuniti, 1960)

Ruggiu, Luigi, *Lo Spirito è Tempo. Saggi su Hegel* (Milan: Mimesis 2013)

Ruhle, Volker, *Verwandlung der Metaphysik. Zur systematischen Darstellung des Absoluten bei Hegel* (München: Fink, 1989)

Salvucci, Pasquale, *Lezioni sulla Hegeliana Flosofia del Diritto. La Società Civile* (Milan: Guerini, 2000)

Schmitt, Carl, *The Concept of the Political* (Chicago: Chicago University Press, 2008)

Sciacca, Fabrizio, *Imago Libertatis. Diritto e Stato nella filosofia dello spirito di Hegel* (Turin: Giappichelli, 1996)

Siebert, Rudolf J., *Hegel's Concept of Marriage and Family. The Origin of Subjective Freedom* (New York: Edwin Mellen Press, 1998)

Siep, Ludwig, *Anerkennung als Prinzip der praktischen Philosophie. Untersuchungen zu Hegels Jenaer Philosophie des Geistes* (Freiburg: Alber, 1979)

Smith, Adam, *The Wealth of Nations* (London: Penguin, 2003)

Smith, Steven B., *Hegel's Critique of Liberalism: Rights in Context* (Chicago: University of Chicago Press, 1989)

Tagliavia, Grazia, *La storia come Fenomenologia dell'Assoluto in Hegel* (Palermo: L'Epos, 1995)

Tommasi, Wanda, *La Natura e la Macchina. Hegel sull'Economia e le Scienze* (Naples: Liguori, 1979)

Tronti, Mario, *Hegel Politico* (Rome: Istituto dell'Enciclopedia Italiana 1975)

Vasta, Giuseppe, *Storicità e Metastoricità dell'Alienazione nella Fenomenologia dello Spirito di G.W. Hegel* (Palermo: ILA, 1987)

Vieillard-Baron, Jean-Louis and Yves Charles Zarka (ed.), *Hegel et le Droit Naturel Moderne* (Paris: Vrin, 2006)

Vieillard-Baron, Jean-Louis, *Hegel, Penseur du Politique* (Paris: Le Félin, 2006)

Waszek, Norbert, *The Scottish Enlightenment and Hegel's Account of Civil Society* (Dordrech: Kluwer, 1988)

Williams, Robert R., *Hegel's Ethics of Recognition* (London: University of California Press, 1997)

---------------------- *Recognition. Fichte and Hegel on the Other* (Albany: State University of New York, 1992)
Wood, Allen W., *Hegel's Ethical Thought* (Cambridge: Cambridge University Press, 1990)

Žižek, Slavoj, *First As Tragedy, then As Farce* (London: Verso, 2009)
-------------- *In Defense of Lost Causes* (London: Verso, 2008)

Index

www.ingramcontent.com/pod-product-compliance
Lightning Source LLC
LaVergne TN
LVHW101504200926
848483LV00001B/224
* 9 7 8 1 9 1 2 1 4 2 2 1 7 *